ISBN: 9781407647180

Published by:
HardPress Publishing
8345 NW 66TH ST #2561
MIAMI FL 33166-2626

Email: info@hardpress.net
Web: http://www.hardpress.net

The Bible,
King James version,
Book 2: Exodus

by

Anonymous

TABLE OF CONTENTS

Book 2

Exodus

02:001:001 Now these are the names of the children of Israel, which came into Egypt; every man and his household came with Jacob.

02:001:002 Reuben, Simeon, Levi, and Judah,

02:001:003 Issachar, Zebulun, and Benjamin,

02:001:004 Dan, and Naphtali, Gad, and Asher.

02:001:005 And all the souls that came out of the loins of Jacob were seventy souls: for Joseph was in Egypt already.

02:001:006 And Joseph died, and all his brethren, and all that generation.

02:001:007 And the children of Israel were fruitful, and increased abundantly, and multiplied, and waxed exceeding mighty; and the land was filled with them.

02:001:008 Now there arose up a new king over Egypt, which knew not Joseph.

02:001:009 And he said unto his people, Behold, the people of the children of Israel are more and mightier than we:

02:001:010 Come on, let us deal wisely with them; lest they multiply, and it come to pass, that, when there falleth out any war, they join also unto our enemies, and fight against us, and so get them up out of the land.

02:001:011 Therefore they did set over them taskmasters to afflict them with their burdens. And they built for Pharaoh treasure cities, Pithom and Raamses.

02:001:012 But the more they afflicted them, the more they multiplied and grew. And they were grieved because of the children of Israel.

02:001:013 And the Egyptians made the children of Israel to serve with
rigour:

02:001:014 And they made their lives bitter with hard bondage, in morter,
and in brick, and in all manner of service in the field: all
their service, wherein they made them serve, was with rigour.

02:001:015 And the king of Egypt spake to the Hebrew midwives, of which
the name of the one was Shiphrah, and the name of the other
Puah:

02:001:016 And he said, When ye do the office of a midwife to the Hebrew
women, and see them upon the stools; if it be a son, then ye
shall kill him: but if it be a daughter, then she shall live.

02:001:017 But the midwives feared God, and did not as the king of Egypt
commanded them, but saved the men children alive.

02:001:018 And the king of Egypt called for the midwives, and said unto
them, Why have ye done this thing, and have saved the men
children alive?

02:001:019 And the midwives said unto Pharaoh, Because the Hebrew women
are not as the Egyptian women; for they are lively, and are
delivered ere the midwives come in unto them.

02:001:020 Therefore God dealt well with the midwives: and the people
multiplied, and waxed very mighty.

02:001:021 And it came to pass, because the midwives feared God, that he
made them houses.

02:001:022 And Pharaoh charged all his people, saying, Every son that is
born ye shall cast into the river, and every daughter ye shall
save alive.

02:002:001 And there went a man of the house of Levi, and took to wife a
daughter of Levi.

02:002:002 And the woman conceived, and bare a son: and when she saw him that he was a goodly child, she hid him three months.

02:002:003 And when she could not longer hide him, she took for him an ark of bulrushes, and daubed it with slime and with pitch, and put the child therein; and she laid it in the flags by the river's brink.

02:002:004 And his sister stood afar off, to wit what would be done to him.

02:002:005 And the daughter of Pharaoh came down to wash herself at the river; and her maidens walked along by the river's side; and when she saw the ark among the flags, she sent her maid to fetch it.

02:002:006 And when she had opened it, she saw the child: and, behold, the babe wept. And she had compassion on him, and said, This is one of the Hebrews' children.

02:002:007 Then said his sister to Pharaoh's daughter, Shall I go and call to thee a nurse of the Hebrew women, that she may nurse the child for thee?

02:002:008 And Pharaoh's daughter said to her, Go. And the maid went and called the child's mother.

02:002:009 And Pharaoh's daughter said unto her, Take this child away, and nurse it for me, and I will give thee thy wages. And the women took the child, and nursed it.

02:002:010 And the child grew, and she brought him unto Pharaoh's daughter, and he became her son. And she called his name Moses: and she said, Because I drew him out of the water.

02:002:011 And it came to pass in those days, when Moses was grown, that he went out unto his brethren, and looked on their burdens: and he spied an Egyptian smiting an Hebrew, one of his brethren.

02:002:012 And he looked this way and that way, and when he saw that
there was no man, he slew the Egyptian, and hid him in the
sand.

02:002:013 And when he went out the second day, behold, two men of the
Hebrews strove together: and he said to him that did the
wrong, Wherefore smitest thou thy fellow?

02:002:014 And he said, Who made thee a prince and a judge over us?
intendest thou to kill me, as thou killedst the Egyptian? And
Moses feared, and said, Surely this thing is known.

02:002:015 Now when Pharaoh heard this thing, he sought to slay Moses.
But Moses fled from the face of Pharaoh, and dwelt in the land
of Midian: and he sat down by a well.

02:002:016 Now the priest of Midian had seven daughters: and they came
and drew water, and filled the troughs to water their father's
flock.

02:002:017 And the shepherds came and drove them away: but Moses stood up
and helped them, and watered their flock.

02:002:018 And when they came to Reuel their father, he said, How is it
that ye are come so soon to day?

02:002:019 And they said, An Egyptian delivered us out of the hand of the
shepherds, and also drew water enough for us, and watered the
flock.

02:002:020 And he said unto his daughters, And where is he? why is it
that ye have left the man? call him, that he may eat bread.

02:002:021 And Moses was content to dwell with the man: and he gave Moses
Zipporah his daughter.

02:002:022 And she bare him a son, and he called his name Gershom: for he
said, I have been a stranger in a strange land.

02:002:023 And it came to pass in process of time, that the king of Egypt died: and the children of Israel sighed by reason of the bondage, and they cried, and their cry came up unto God by reason of the bondage.

02:002:024 And God heard their groaning, and God remembered his covenant with Abraham, with Isaac, and with Jacob.

02:002:025 And God looked upon the children of Israel, and God had respect unto them.

02:003:001 Now Moses kept the flock of Jethro his father in law, the priest of Midian: and he led the flock to the backside of the desert, and came to the mountain of God, even to Horeb.

02:003:002 And the angel of the LORD appeared unto him in a flame of fire out of the midst of a bush: and he looked, and, behold, the bush burned with fire, and the bush was not consumed.

02:003:003 And Moses said, I will now turn aside, and see this great sight, why the bush is not burnt.

02:003:004 And when the LORD saw that he turned aside to see, God called unto him out of the midst of the bush, and said, Moses, Moses. And he said, Here am I.

02:003:005 And he said, Draw not nigh hither: put off thy shoes from off thy feet, for the place whereon thou standest is holy ground.

02:003:006 Moreover he said, I am the God of thy father, the God of Abraham, the God of Isaac, and the God of Jacob. And Moses hid his face; for he was afraid to look upon God.

02:003:007 And the LORD said, I have surely seen the affliction of my people which are in Egypt, and have heard their cry by reason of their taskmasters; for I know their sorrows;

02:003:008 And I am come down to deliver them out of the hand of the Egyptians, and to bring them up out of that land unto a good land and a large, unto a land flowing with milk and honey; unto the place of the Canaanites, and the Hittites, and the Amorites, and the Perizzites, and the Hivites, and the Jebusites.

02:003:009 Now therefore, behold, the cry of the children of Israel is come unto me: and I have also seen the oppression wherewith the Egyptians oppress them.

02:003:010 Come now therefore, and I will send thee unto Pharaoh, that thou mayest bring forth my people the children of Israel out of Egypt.

02:003:011 And Moses said unto God, Who am I, that I should go unto Pharaoh, and that I should bring forth the children of Israel out of Egypt?

02:003:012 And he said, Certainly I will be with thee; and this shall be a token unto thee, that I have sent thee: When thou hast brought forth the people out of Egypt, ye shall serve God upon this mountain.

02:003:013 And Moses said unto God, Behold, when I come unto the children of Israel, and shall say unto them, The God of your fathers hath sent me unto you; and they shall say to me, What is his name? what shall I say unto them?

02:003:014 And God said unto Moses, I AM THAT I AM: and he said, Thus shalt thou say unto the children of Israel, I AM hath sent me unto you.

02:003:015 And God said moreover unto Moses, Thus shalt thou say unto the children of Israel, the LORD God of your fathers, the God of Abraham, the God of Isaac, and the God of Jacob, hath sent me unto you: this is my name for ever, and this is my memorial unto all generations.

02:003:016 Go, and gather the elders of Israel together, and say unto

them, The LORD God of your fathers, the God of Abraham, of
Isaac, and of Jacob, appeared unto me, saying, I have surely
visited you, and seen that which is done to you in Egypt:

02:003:017 And I have said, I will bring you up out of the affliction of
Egypt unto the land of the Canaanites, and the Hittites, and
the Amorites, and the Perizzites, and the Hivites, and the
Jebusites, unto a land flowing with milk and honey.

02:003:018 And they shall hearken to thy voice: and thou shalt come, thou
and the elders of Israel, unto the king of Egypt, and ye shall
say unto him, The LORD God of the Hebrews hath met with us:
and now let us go, we beseech thee, three days' journey into
the wilderness, that we may sacrifice to the LORD our God.

02:003:019 And I am sure that the king of Egypt will not let you go, no,
not by a mighty hand.

02:003:020 And I will stretch out my hand, and smite Egypt with all my
wonders which I will do in the midst thereof: and after that
he will let you go.

02:003:021 And I will give this people favour in the sight of the
Egyptians: and it shall come to pass, that, when ye go, ye
shall not go empty.

02:003:022 But every woman shall borrow of her neighbour, and of her that
sojourneth in her house, jewels of silver, and jewels of gold,
and raiment: and ye shall put them upon your sons, and upon
your daughters; and ye shall spoil the Egyptians.

02:004:001 And Moses answered and said, But, behold, they will not
believe me, nor hearken unto my voice: for they will say, The
LORD hath not appeared unto thee.

02:004:002 And the LORD said unto him, What is that in thine hand? And he
said, A rod.

02:004:003 And he said, Cast it on the ground. And he cast it on the

ground, and it became a serpent; and Moses fled from before
it.

02:004:004 And the LORD said unto Moses, Put forth thine hand, and take
it by the tail. And he put forth his hand, and caught it, and
it became a rod in his hand:

02:004:005 That they may believe that the LORD God of their fathers, the
God of Abraham, the God of Isaac, and the God of Jacob, hath
appeared unto thee.

02:004:006 And the LORD said furthermore unto him, Put now thine hand
into thy bosom. And he put his hand into his bosom: and when
he took it out, behold, his hand was leprous as snow.

02:004:007 And he said, Put thine hand into thy bosom again. And he put
his hand into his bosom again; and plucked it out of his
bosom, and, behold, it was turned again as his other flesh.

02:004:008 And it shall come to pass, if they will not believe thee,
neither hearken to the voice of the first sign, that they will
believe the voice of the latter sign.

02:004:009 And it shall come to pass, if they will not believe also these
two signs, neither hearken unto thy voice, that thou shalt
take of the water of the river, and pour it upon the dry land:
and the water which thou takest out of the river shall become
blood upon the dry land.

02:004:010 And Moses said unto the LORD, O my LORD, I am not eloquent,
neither heretofore, nor since thou hast spoken unto thy
servant: but I am slow of speech, and of a slow tongue.

02:004:011 And the LORD said unto him, Who hath made man's mouth? or who
maketh the dumb, or deaf, or the seeing, or the blind? have
not I the LORD?

02:004:012 Now therefore go, and I will be with thy mouth, and teach thee
what thou shalt say.

02:004:013 And he said, O my LORD, send, I pray thee, by the hand of him whom thou wilt send.

02:004:014 And the anger of the LORD was kindled against Moses, and he said, Is not Aaron the Levite thy brother? I know that he can speak well. And also, behold, he cometh forth to meet thee: and when he seeth thee, he will be glad in his heart.

02:004:015 And thou shalt speak unto him, and put words in his mouth: and I will be with thy mouth, and with his mouth, and will teach you what ye shall do.

02:004:016 And he shall be thy spokesman unto the people: and he shall be, even he shall be to thee instead of a mouth, and thou shalt be to him instead of God.

02:004:017 And thou shalt take this rod in thine hand, wherewith thou shalt do signs.

02:004:018 And Moses went and returned to Jethro his father in law, and said unto him, Let me go, I pray thee, and return unto my brethren which are in Egypt, and see whether they be yet alive. And Jethro said to Moses, Go in peace.

02:004:019 And the LORD said unto Moses in Midian, Go, return into Egypt: for all the men are dead which sought thy life.

02:004:020 And Moses took his wife and his sons, and set them upon an ass, and he returned to the land of Egypt: and Moses took the rod of God in his hand.

02:004:021 And the LORD said unto Moses, When thou goest to return into Egypt, see that thou do all those wonders before Pharaoh, which I have put in thine hand: but I will harden his heart, that he shall not let the people go.

02:004:022 And thou shalt say unto Pharaoh, Thus saith the LORD, Israel is my son, even my firstborn:

02:004:023 And I say unto thee, Let my son go, that he may serve me: and if thou refuse to let him go, behold, I will slay thy son,
even thy firstborn.

02:004:024 And it came to pass by the way in the inn, that the LORD met him, and sought to kill him.

02:004:025 Then Zipporah took a sharp stone, and cut off the foreskin of her son, and cast it at his feet, and said, Surely a bloody
husband art thou to me.

02:004:026 So he let him go: then she said, A bloody husband thou art, because of the circumcision.

02:004:027 And the LORD said to Aaron, Go into the wilderness to meet Moses. And he went, and met him in the mount of God, and
kissed him.

02:004:028 And Moses told Aaron all the words of the LORD who had sent him, and all the signs which he had commanded him.

02:004:029 And Moses and Aaron went and gathered together all the elders of the children of Israel:

02:004:030 And Aaron spake all the words which the LORD had spoken unto Moses, and did the signs in the sight of the people.

02:004:031 And the people believed: and when they heard that the LORD had visited the children of Israel, and that he had looked upon
their affliction, then they bowed their heads and worshipped.

02:005:001 And afterward Moses and Aaron went in, and told Pharaoh, Thus saith the LORD God of Israel, Let my people go, that they may
hold a feast unto me in the wilderness.

02:005:002 And Pharaoh said, Who is the LORD, that I should obey his voice to let Israel go? I know not the LORD, neither will I
let Israel go.

02:005:003 And they said, The God of the Hebrews hath met with us: let us go, we pray thee, three days' journey into the desert, and sacrifice unto the LORD our God; lest he fall upon us with pestilence, or with the sword.

02:005:004 And the king of Egypt said unto them, Wherefore do ye, Moses and Aaron, let the people from their works? get you unto your burdens.

02:005:005 And Pharaoh said, Behold, the people of the land now are many, and ye make them rest from their burdens.

02:005:006 And Pharaoh commanded the same day the taskmasters of the people, and their officers, saying,

02:005:007 Ye shall no more give the people straw to make brick, as heretofore: let them go and gather straw for themselves.

02:005:008 And the tale of the bricks, which they did make heretofore, ye shall lay upon them; ye shall not diminish ought thereof: for they be idle; therefore they cry, saying, Let us go and sacrifice to our God.

02:005:009 Let there more work be laid upon the men, that they may labour therein; and let them not regard vain words.

02:005:010 And the taskmasters of the people went out, and their officers, and they spake to the people, saying, Thus saith Pharaoh, I will not give you straw.

02:005:011 Go ye, get you straw where ye can find it: yet not ought of your work shall be diminished.

02:005:012 So the people were scattered abroad throughout all the land of Egypt to gather stubble instead of straw.

02:005:013 And the taskmasters hasted them, saying, Fulfil your works, your daily tasks, as when there was straw.

02:005:014 And the officers of the children of Israel, which Pharaoh's
taskmasters had set over them, were beaten, and demanded,
Wherefore have ye not fulfilled your task in making brick both
yesterday and to day, as heretofore?

02:005:015 Then the officers of the children of Israel came and cried
unto Pharaoh, saying, Wherefore dealest thou thus with thy
servants?

02:005:016 There is no straw given unto thy servants, and they say to us,
Make brick: and, behold, thy servants are beaten; but the
fault is in thine own people.

02:005:017 But he said, Ye are idle, ye are idle: therefore ye say, Let
us go and do sacrifice to the LORD.

02:005:018 Go therefore now, and work; for there shall no straw be given
you, yet shall ye deliver the tale of bricks.

02:005:019 And the officers of the children of Israel did see that they
were in evil case, after it was said, Ye shall not minish
ought from your bricks of your daily task.

02:005:020 And they met Moses and Aaron, who stood in the way, as they
came forth from Pharaoh:

02:005:021 And they said unto them, The LORD look upon you, and judge;
because ye have made our savour to be abhorred in the eyes of
Pharaoh, and in the eyes of his servants, to put a sword in
their hand to slay us.

02:005:022 And Moses returned unto the LORD, and said, LORD, wherefore
hast thou so evil entreated this people? why is it that thou
hast sent me?

02:005:023 For since I came to Pharaoh to speak in thy name, he hath done
evil to this people; neither hast thou delivered thy people at
all.

02:006:001 Then the LORD said unto Moses, Now shalt thou see what I will do to Pharaoh: for with a strong hand shall he let them go, and with a strong hand shall he drive them out of his land.

02:006:002 And God spake unto Moses, and said unto him, I am the LORD:

02:006:003 And I appeared unto Abraham, unto Isaac, and unto Jacob, by the name of God Almighty, but by my name JEHOVAH was I not known to them.

02:006:004 And I have also established my covenant with them, to give them the land of Canaan, the land of their pilgrimage, wherein they were strangers.

02:006:005 And I have also heard the groaning of the children of Israel, whom the Egyptians keep in bondage; and I have remembered my covenant.

02:006:006 Wherefore say unto the children of Israel, I am the LORD, and I will bring you out from under the burdens of the Egyptians, and I will rid you out of their bondage, and I will redeem you with a stretched out arm, and with great judgments:

02:006:007 And I will take you to me for a people, and I will be to you a God: and ye shall know that I am the LORD your God, which bringeth you out from under the burdens of the Egyptians.

02:006:008 And I will bring you in unto the land, concerning the which I did swear to give it to Abraham, to Isaac, and to Jacob; and I will give it you for an heritage: I am the LORD.

02:006:009 And Moses spake so unto the children of Israel: but they hearkened not unto Moses for anguish of spirit, and for cruel bondage.

02:006:010 And the LORD spake unto Moses, saying,

02:006:011 Go in, speak unto Pharaoh king of Egypt, that he let the children of Israel go out of his land.

02:006:012 And Moses spake before the LORD, saying, Behold, the children of Israel have not hearkened unto me; how then shall Pharaoh hear me, who am of uncircumcised lips?

02:006:013 And the LORD spake unto Moses and unto Aaron, and gave them a charge unto the children of Israel, and unto Pharaoh king of Egypt, to bring the children of Israel out of the land of Egypt.

02:006:014 These be the heads of their fathers' houses: The sons of Reuben the firstborn of Israel; Hanoch, and Pallu, Hezron, and Carmi: these be the families of Reuben.

02:006:015 And the sons of Simeon; Jemuel, and Jamin, and Ohad, and Jachin, and Zohar, and Shaul the son of a Canaanitish woman: these are the families of Simeon.

02:006:016 And these are the names of the sons of Levi according to their generations; Gershon, and Kohath, and Merari: and the years of the life of Levi were an hundred thirty and seven years.

02:006:017 The sons of Gershon; Libni, and Shimi, according to their families.

02:006:018 And the sons of Kohath; Amram, and Izhar, and Hebron, and Uzziel: and the years of the life of Kohath were an hundred thirty and three years.

02:006:019 And the sons of Merari; Mahali and Mushi: these are the families of Levi according to their generations.

02:006:020 And Amram took him Jochebed his father's sister to wife; and she bare him Aaron and Moses: and the years of the life of Amram were an hundred and thirty and seven years.

02:006:021 And the sons of Izhar; Korah, and Nepheg, and Zichri.

02:006:022 And the sons of Uzziel; Mishael, and Elzaphan, and Zithri.

02:006:023 And Aaron took him Elisheba, daughter of Amminadab, sister of Naashon, to wife; and she bare him Nadab, and Abihu, Eleazar, and Ithamar.

02:006:024 And the sons of Korah; Assir, and Elkanah, and Abiasaph: these are the families of the Korhites.

02:006:025 And Eleazar Aaron's son took him one of the daughters of Putiel to wife; and she bare him Phinehas: these are the heads of the fathers of the Levites according to their families.

02:006:026 These are that Aaron and Moses, to whom the LORD said, Bring out the children of Israel from the land of Egypt according to their armies.

02:006:027 These are they which spake to Pharaoh king of Egypt, to bring out the children of Israel from Egypt: these are that Moses and Aaron.

02:006:028 And it came to pass on the day when the LORD spake unto Moses in the land of Egypt,

02:006:029 That the LORD spake unto Moses, saying, I am the LORD: speak thou unto Pharaoh king of Egypt all that I say unto thee.

02:006:030 And Moses said before the LORD, Behold, I am of uncircumcised lips, and how shall Pharaoh hearken unto me?

02:007:001 And the LORD said unto Moses, See, I have made thee a god to Pharaoh: and Aaron thy brother shall be thy prophet.

02:007:002 Thou shalt speak all that I command thee: and Aaron thy brother shall speak unto Pharaoh, that he send the children of Israel out of his land.

02:007:003 And I will harden Pharaoh's heart, and multiply my signs and my wonders in the land of Egypt.

02:007:004 But Pharaoh shall not hearken unto you, that I may lay my hand

upon Egypt, and bring forth mine armies, and my people the
children of Israel, out of the land of Egypt by great
judgments.

02:007:005 And the Egyptians shall know that I am the LORD, when I
stretch forth mine hand upon Egypt, and bring out the children
of Israel from among them.

02:007:006 And Moses and Aaron did as the LORD commanded them, so did
they.

02:007:007 And Moses was fourscore years old, and Aaron fourscore and
three years old, when they spake unto Pharaoh.

02:007:008 And the LORD spake unto Moses and unto Aaron, saying,

02:007:009 When Pharaoh shall speak unto you, saying, Shew a miracle for
you: then thou shalt say unto Aaron, Take thy rod, and cast it
before Pharaoh, and it shall become a serpent.

02:007:010 And Moses and Aaron went in unto Pharaoh, and they did so as
the LORD had commanded: and Aaron cast down his rod before
Pharaoh, and before his servants, and it became a serpent.

02:007:011 Then Pharaoh also called the wise men and the sorcerers: now
the magicians of Egypt, they also did in like manner with
their enchantments.

02:007:012 For they cast down every man his rod, and they became
serpents: but Aaron's rod swallowed up their rods.

02:007:013 And he hardened Pharaoh's heart, that he hearkened not unto
them; as the LORD had said.

02:007:014 And the LORD said unto Moses, Pharaoh's heart is hardened, he
refuseth to let the people go.

02:007:015 Get thee unto Pharaoh in the morning; lo, he goeth out unto
the water; and thou shalt stand by the river's brink against

he come; and the rod which was turned to a serpent shalt thou
take in thine hand.

02:007:016 And thou shalt say unto him, The LORD God of the Hebrews hath
sent me unto thee, saying, Let my people go, that they may
serve me in the wilderness: and, behold, hitherto thou
wouldest not hear.

02:007:017 Thus saith the LORD, In this thou shalt know that I am the
LORD: behold, I will smite with the rod that is in mine hand
upon the waters which are in the river, and they shall be
turned to blood.

02:007:018 And the fish that is in the river shall die, and the river
shall stink; and the Egyptians shall lothe to drink of the
water of the river.

02:007:019 And the LORD spake unto Moses, Say unto Aaron, Take thy rod,
and stretch out thine hand upon the waters of Egypt, upon
their streams, upon their rivers, and upon their ponds, and
upon all their pools of water, that they may become blood; and
that there may be blood throughout all the land of Egypt, both
in vessels of wood, and in vessels of stone.

02:007:020 And Moses and Aaron did so, as the LORD commanded; and he
lifted up the rod, and smote the waters that were in the
river, in the sight of Pharaoh, and in the sight of his
servants; and all the waters that were in the river were
turned to blood.

02:007:021 And the fish that was in the river died; and the river stank,
and the Egyptians could not drink of the water of the river;
and there was blood throughout all the land of Egypt.

02:007:022 And the magicians of Egypt did so with their enchantments: and
Pharaoh's heart was hardened, neither did he hearken unto
them; as the LORD had said.

02:007:023 And Pharaoh turned and went into his house, neither did he set his heart to this also.

02:007:024 And all the Egyptians digged round about the river for water to drink; for they could not drink of the water of the river.

02:007:025 And seven days were fulfilled, after that the LORD had smitten the river.

02:008:001 And the LORD spake unto Moses, Go unto Pharaoh, and say unto him, Thus saith the LORD, Let my people go, that they may serve me.

02:008:002 And if thou refuse to let them go, behold, I will smite all thy borders with frogs:

02:008:003 And the river shall bring forth frogs abundantly, which shall go up and come into thine house, and into thy bedchamber, and upon thy bed, and into the house of thy servants, and upon thy people, and into thine ovens, and into thy kneadingtroughs:

02:008:004 And the frogs shall come up both on thee, and upon thy people, and upon all thy servants.

02:008:005 And the LORD spake unto Moses, Say unto Aaron, Stretch forth thine hand with thy rod over the streams, over the rivers, and over the ponds, and cause frogs to come up upon the land of Egypt.

02:008:006 And Aaron stretched out his hand over the waters of Egypt; and the frogs came up, and covered the land of Egypt.

02:008:007 And the magicians did so with their enchantments, and brought up frogs upon the land of Egypt.

02:008:008 Then Pharaoh called for Moses and Aaron, and said, Intreat the LORD, that he may take away the frogs from me, and from my people; and I will let the people go, that they may do sacrifice unto the LORD.

02:008:009 And Moses said unto Pharaoh, Glory over me: when shall I intreat for thee, and for thy servants, and for thy people, to destroy the frogs from thee and thy houses, that they may remain in the river only?

02:008:010 And he said, To morrow. And he said, Be it according to thy word: that thou mayest know that there is none like unto the LORD our God.

02:008:011 And the frogs shall depart from thee, and from thy houses, and from thy servants, and from thy people; they shall remain in the river only.

02:008:012 And Moses and Aaron went out from Pharaoh: and Moses cried unto the LORD because of the frogs which he had brought against Pharaoh.

02:008:013 And the LORD did according to the word of Moses; and the frogs died out of the houses, out of the villages, and out of the fields.

02:008:014 And they gathered them together upon heaps: and the land stank.

02:008:015 But when Pharaoh saw that there was respite, he hardened his heart, and hearkened not unto them; as the LORD had said.

02:008:016 And the LORD said unto Moses, Say unto Aaron, Stretch out thy rod, and smite the dust of the land, that it may become lice throughout all the land of Egypt.

02:008:017 And they did so; for Aaron stretched out his hand with his rod, and smote the dust of the earth, and it became lice in man, and in beast; all the dust of the land became lice throughout all the land of Egypt.

02:008:018 And the magicians did so with their enchantments to bring forth lice, but they could not: so there were lice upon man, and upon beast.

02:008:019 Then the magicians said unto Pharaoh, This is the finger of God: and Pharaoh's heart was hardened, and he hearkened not unto them; as the LORD had said.

02:008:020 And the LORD said unto Moses, Rise up early in the morning, and stand before Pharaoh; lo, he cometh forth to the water; and say unto him, Thus saith the LORD, Let my people go, that they may serve me.

02:008:021 Else, if thou wilt not let my people go, behold, I will send swarms of flies upon thee, and upon thy servants, and upon thy people, and into thy houses: and the houses of the Egyptians shall be full of swarms of flies, and also the ground whereon they are.

02:008:022 And I will sever in that day the land of Goshen, in which my people dwell, that no swarms of flies shall be there; to the end thou mayest know that I am the LORD in the midst of the earth.

02:008:023 And I will put a division between my people and thy people: to morrow shall this sign be.

02:008:024 And the LORD did so; and there came a grievous swarm of flies into the house of Pharaoh, and into his servants' houses, and into all the land of Egypt: the land was corrupted by reason of the swarm of flies.

02:008:025 And Pharaoh called for Moses and for Aaron, and said, Go ye, sacrifice to your God in the land.

02:008:026 And Moses said, It is not meet so to do; for we shall sacrifice the abomination of the Egyptians to the LORD our God: lo, shall we sacrifice the abomination of the Egyptians before their eyes, and will they not stone us?

02:008:027 We will go three days' journey into the wilderness, and sacrifice to the LORD our God, as he shall command us.

02:008:028 And Pharaoh said, I will let you go, that ye may sacrifice to the LORD your God in the wilderness; only ye shall not go very far away: intreat for me.

02:008:029 And Moses said, Behold, I go out from thee, and I will intreat the LORD that the swarms of flies may depart from Pharaoh, from his servants, and from his people, to morrow: but let not Pharaoh deal deceitfully any more in not letting the people go to sacrifice to the LORD.

02:008:030 And Moses went out from Pharaoh, and intreated the LORD.

02:008:031 And the LORD did according to the word of Moses; and he removed the swarms of flies from Pharaoh, from his servants, and from his people; there remained not one.

02:008:032 And Pharaoh hardened his heart at this time also, neither would he let the people go.

02:009:001 Then the LORD said unto Moses, Go in unto Pharaoh, and tell him, Thus saith the LORD God of the Hebrews, Let my people go, that they may serve me.

02:009:002 For if thou refuse to let them go, and wilt hold them still,

02:009:003 Behold, the hand of the LORD is upon thy cattle which is in the field, upon the horses, upon the asses, upon the camels, upon the oxen, and upon the sheep: there shall be a very grievous murrain.

02:009:004 And the LORD shall sever between the cattle of Israel and the cattle of Egypt: and there shall nothing die of all that is the children's of Israel.

02:009:005 And the LORD appointed a set time, saying, To morrow the LORD shall do this thing in the land.

02:009:006 And the LORD did that thing on the morrow, and all the cattle of Egypt died: but of the cattle of the children of Israel died not one.

02:009:007 And Pharaoh sent, and, behold, there was not one of the cattle
of the Israelites dead. And the heart of Pharaoh was hardened,
and he did not let the people go.

02:009:008 And the LORD said unto Moses and unto Aaron, Take to you
handfuls of ashes of the furnace, and let Moses sprinkle it
toward the heaven in the sight of Pharaoh.

02:009:009 And it shall become small dust in all the land of Egypt, and
shall be a boil breaking forth with blains upon man, and upon
beast, throughout all the land of Egypt.

02:009:010 And they took ashes of the furnace, and stood before Pharaoh;
and Moses sprinkled it up toward heaven; and it became a boil
breaking forth with blains upon man, and upon beast.

02:009:011 And the magicians could not stand before Moses because of the
boils; for the boil was upon the magicians, and upon all the
Egyptians.

02:009:012 And the LORD hardened the heart of Pharaoh, and he hearkened
not unto them; as the LORD had spoken unto Moses.

02:009:013 And the LORD said unto Moses, Rise up early in the morning,
and stand before Pharaoh, and say unto him, Thus saith the
LORD God of the Hebrews, Let my people go, that they may serve
me.

02:009:014 For I will at this time send all my plagues upon thine heart,
and upon thy servants, and upon thy people; that thou mayest
know that there is none like me in all the earth.

02:009:015 For now I will stretch out my hand, that I may smite thee and
thy people with pestilence; and thou shalt be cut off from the
earth.

02:009:016 And in very deed for this cause have I raised thee up, for to

shew in thee my power; and that my name may be declared
throughout all the earth.

02:009:017 As yet exaltest thou thyself against my people, that thou wilt
not let them go?

02:009:018 Behold, to morrow about this time I will cause it to rain a
very grievous hail, such as hath not been in Egypt since the
foundation thereof even until now.

02:009:019 Send therefore now, and gather thy cattle, and all that thou
hast in the field; for upon every man and beast which shall be
found in the field, and shall not be brought home, the hail
shall come down upon them, and they shall die.

02:009:020 He that feared the word of the LORD among the servants of
Pharaoh made his servants and his cattle flee into the houses:

02:009:021 And he that regarded not the word of the LORD left his
servants and his cattle in the field.

02:009:022 And the LORD said unto Moses, Stretch forth thine hand toward
heaven, that there may be hail in all the land of Egypt, upon
man, and upon beast, and upon every herb of the field,
throughout the land of Egypt.

02:009:023 And Moses stretched forth his rod toward heaven: and the LORD
sent thunder and hail, and the fire ran along upon the ground;
and the LORD rained hail upon the land of Egypt.

02:009:024 So there was hail, and fire mingled with the hail, very
grievous, such as there was none like it in all the land of
Egypt since it became a nation.

02:009:025 And the hail smote throughout all the land of Egypt all that
was in the field, both man and beast; and the hail smote every
herb of the field, and brake every tree of the field.

02:009:026 Only in the land of Goshen, where the children of Israel were, was there no hail.

02:009:027 And Pharaoh sent, and called for Moses and Aaron, and said
unto them, I have sinned this time: the LORD is righteous, and
I and my people are wicked.

02:009:028 Intreat the LORD (for it is enough) that there be no more
mighty thunderings and hail; and I will let you go, and ye
shall stay no longer.

02:009:029 And Moses said unto him, As soon as I am gone out of the city,
I will spread abroad my hands unto the LORD; and the thunder
shall cease, neither shall there be any more hail; that thou
mayest know how that the earth is the LORD's.

02:009:030 But as for thee and thy servants, I know that ye will not yet
fear the LORD God.

02:009:031 And the flax and the barley was smitten: for the barley was in
the ear, and the flax was bolled.

02:009:032 But the wheat and the rie were not smitten: for they were not
grown up.

02:009:033 And Moses went out of the city from Pharaoh, and spread abroad
his hands unto the LORD: and the thunders and hail ceased, and
the rain was not poured upon the earth.

02:009:034 And when Pharaoh saw that the rain and the hail and the
thunders were ceased, he sinned yet more, and hardened his
heart, he and his servants.

02:009:035 And the heart of Pharaoh was hardened, neither would he let
the children of Israel go; as the LORD had spoken by Moses.

02:010:001 And the LORD said unto Moses, Go in unto Pharaoh: for I have
hardened his heart, and the heart of his servants, that I
might shew these my signs before him:

02:010:002 And that thou mayest tell in the ears of thy son, and of thy
son's son, what things I have wrought in Egypt, and my signs
which I have done among them; that ye may know how that I am
the LORD.

02:010:003 And Moses and Aaron came in unto Pharaoh, and said unto him,
Thus saith the LORD God of the Hebrews, How long wilt thou
refuse to humble thyself before me? let my people go, that
they may serve me.

02:010:004 Else, if thou refuse to let my people go, behold, to morrow
will I bring the locusts into thy coast:

02:010:005 And they shall cover the face of the earth, that one cannot be
able to see the earth: and they shall eat the residue of that
which is escaped, which remaineth unto you from the hail, and
shall eat every tree which groweth for you out of the field:

02:010:006 And they shall fill thy houses, and the houses of all thy
servants, and the houses of all the Egyptians; which neither
thy fathers, nor thy fathers' fathers have seen, since the day
that they were upon the earth unto this day. And he turned
himself, and went out from Pharaoh.

02:010:007 And Pharaoh's servants said unto him, How long shall this man
be a snare unto us? let the men go, that they may serve the
LORD their God: knowest thou not yet that Egypt is destroyed?

02:010:008 And Moses and Aaron were brought again unto Pharaoh: and he
said unto them, Go, serve the LORD your God: but who are they
that shall go?

02:010:009 And Moses said, We will go with our young and with our old,
with our sons and with our daughters, with our flocks and with
our herds will we go; for we must hold a feast unto the LORD.

02:010:010 And he said unto them, Let the LORD be so with you, as I will
let you go, and your little ones: look to it; for evil is

before you.

02:010:011 Not so: go now ye that are men, and serve the LORD; for that ye did desire. And they were driven out from Pharaoh's presence.

02:010:012 And the LORD said unto Moses, Stretch out thine hand over the land of Egypt for the locusts, that they may come up upon the land of Egypt, and eat every herb of the land, even all that the hail hath left.

02:010:013 And Moses stretched forth his rod over the land of Egypt, and the LORD brought an east wind upon the land all that day, and all that night; and when it was morning, the east wind brought the locusts.

02:010:014 And the locust went up over all the land of Egypt, and rested in all the coasts of Egypt: very grievous were they; before them there were no such locusts as they, neither after them shall be such.

02:010:015 For they covered the face of the whole earth, so that the land was darkened; and they did eat every herb of the land, and all the fruit of the trees which the hail had left: and there remained not any green thing in the trees, or in the herbs of the field, through all the land of Egypt.

02:010:016 Then Pharaoh called for Moses and Aaron in haste; and he said, I have sinned against the LORD your God, and against you.

02:010:017 Now therefore forgive, I pray thee, my sin only this once, and intreat the LORD your God, that he may take away from me this death only.

02:010:018 And he went out from Pharaoh, and intreated the LORD.

02:010:019 And the LORD turned a mighty strong west wind, which took away the locusts, and cast them into the Red sea; there remained not one locust in all the coasts of Egypt.

02:010:020 But the LORD hardened Pharaoh's heart, so that he would not let the children of Israel go.

02:010:021 And the LORD said unto Moses, Stretch out thine hand toward heaven, that there may be darkness over the land of Egypt, even darkness which may be felt.

02:010:022 And Moses stretched forth his hand toward heaven; and there was a thick darkness in all the land of Egypt three days:

02:010:023 They saw not one another, neither rose any from his place for three days: but all the children of Israel had light in their dwellings.

02:010:024 And Pharaoh called unto Moses, and said, Go ye, serve the LORD; only let your flocks and your herds be stayed: let your little ones also go with you.

02:010:025 And Moses said, Thou must give us also sacrifices and burnt offerings, that we may sacrifice unto the LORD our God.

02:010:026 Our cattle also shall go with us; there shall not an hoof be left behind; for thereof must we take to serve the LORD our God; and we know not with what we must serve the LORD, until we come thither.

02:010:027 But the LORD hardened Pharaoh's heart, and he would not let them go.

02:010:028 And Pharaoh said unto him, Get thee from me, take heed to thyself, see my face no more; for in that day thou seest my face thou shalt die.

02:010:029 And Moses said, Thou hast spoken well, I will see thy face again no more.

02:011:001 And the LORD said unto Moses, Yet will I bring one plague more upon Pharaoh, and upon Egypt; afterwards he will let you go hence: when he shall let you go, he shall surely thrust you out hence altogether.

02:011:002 Speak now in the ears of the people, and let every man borrow of his neighbour, and every woman of her neighbour, jewels of silver and jewels of gold.

02:011:003 And the LORD gave the people favour in the sight of the Egyptians. Moreover the man Moses was very great in the land of Egypt, in the sight of Pharaoh's servants, and in the sight of the people.

02:011:004 And Moses said, Thus saith the LORD, About midnight will I go out into the midst of Egypt:

02:011:005 And all the firstborn in the land of Egypt shall die, from the first born of Pharaoh that sitteth upon his throne, even unto the firstborn of the maidservant that is behind the mill; and all the firstborn of beasts.

02:011:006 And there shall be a great cry throughout all the land of Egypt, such as there was none like it, nor shall be like it any more.

02:011:007 But against any of the children of Israel shall not a dog move his tongue, against man or beast: that ye may know how that the LORD doth put a difference between the Egyptians and Israel.

02:011:008 And all these thy servants shall come down unto me, and bow down themselves unto me, saying, Get thee out, and all the people that follow thee: and after that I will go out. And he went out from Pharaoh in a great anger.

02:011:009 And the LORD said unto Moses, Pharaoh shall not hearken unto you; that my wonders may be multiplied in the land of Egypt.

02:011:010 And Moses and Aaron did all these wonders before Pharaoh: and the LORD hardened Pharaoh's heart, so that he would not let the children of Israel go out of his land.

02:012:001 And the LORD spake unto Moses and Aaron in the land of Egypt saying,

02:012:002 This month shall be unto you the beginning of months: it shall be the first month of the year to you.

02:012:003 Speak ye unto all the congregation of Israel, saying, In the tenth day of this month they shall take to them every man a lamb, according to the house of their fathers, a lamb for an house:

02:012:004 And if the household be too little for the lamb, let him and his neighbour next unto his house take it according to the number of the souls; every man according to his eating shall make your count for the lamb.

02:012:005 Your lamb shall be without blemish, a male of the first year: ye shall take it out from the sheep, or from the goats:

02:012:006 And ye shall keep it up until the fourteenth day of the same month: and the whole assembly of the congregation of Israel shall kill it in the evening.

02:012:007 And they shall take of the blood, and strike it on the two side posts and on the upper door post of the houses, wherein they shall eat it.

02:012:008 And they shall eat the flesh in that night, roast with fire, and unleavened bread; and with bitter herbs they shall eat it.

02:012:009 Eat not of it raw, nor sodden at all with water, but roast with fire; his head with his legs, and with the purtenance thereof.

02:012:010 And ye shall let nothing of it remain until the morning; and that which remaineth of it until the morning ye shall burn with fire.

02:012:011 And thus shall ye eat it; with your loins girded, your shoes

on your feet, and your staff in your hand; and ye shall eat it
in haste: it is the LORD's passover.

02:012:012 For I will pass through the land of Egypt this night, and will
smite all the firstborn in the land of Egypt, both man and
beast; and against all the gods of Egypt I will execute
judgment: I am the LORD.

02:012:013 And the blood shall be to you for a token upon the houses
where ye are: and when I see the blood, I will pass over you,
and the plague shall not be upon you to destroy you, when I
smite the land of Egypt.

02:012:014 And this day shall be unto you for a memorial; and ye shall
keep it a feast to the LORD throughout your generations; ye
shall keep it a feast by an ordinance for ever.

02:012:015 Seven days shall ye eat unleavened bread; even the first day
ye shall put away leaven out of your houses: for whosoever
eateth leavened bread from the first day until the seventh
day, that soul shall be cut off from Israel.

02:012:016 And in the first day there shall be an holy convocation, and
in the seventh day there shall be an holy convocation to you;
no manner of work shall be done in them, save that which every
man must eat, that only may be done of you.

02:012:017 And ye shall observe the feast of unleavened bread; for in
this selfsame day have I brought your armies out of the land
of Egypt: therefore shall ye observe this day in your
generations by an ordinance for ever.

02:012:018 In the first month, on the fourteenth day of the month at
even, ye shall eat unleavened bread, until the one and
twentieth day of the month at even.

02:012:019 Seven days shall there be no leaven found in your houses: for
whosoever eateth that which is leavened, even that soul shall

be cut off from the congregation of Israel, whether he be a
stranger, or born in the land.

02:012:020 Ye shall eat nothing leavened; in all your habitations shall
ye eat unleavened bread.

02:012:021 Then Moses called for all the elders of Israel, and said unto
them, Draw out and take you a lamb according to your families,
and kill the passover.

02:012:022 And ye shall take a bunch of hyssop, and dip it in the blood
that is in the bason, and strike the lintel and the two side
posts with the blood that is in the bason; and none of you
shall go out at the door of his house until the morning.

02:012:023 For the LORD will pass through to smite the Egyptians; and
when he seeth the blood upon the lintel, and on the two side
posts, the LORD will pass over the door, and will not suffer
the destroyer to come in unto your houses to smite you.

02:012:024 And ye shall observe this thing for an ordinance to thee and
to thy sons for ever.

02:012:025 And it shall come to pass, when ye be come to the land which
the LORD will give you, according as he hath promised, that ye
shall keep this service.

02:012:026 And it shall come to pass, when your children shall say unto
you, What mean ye by this service?

02:012:027 That ye shall say, It is the sacrifice of the LORD's passover,
who passed over the houses of the children of Israel in Egypt,
when he smote the Egyptians, and delivered our houses. And the
people bowed the head and worshipped.

02:012:028 And the children of Israel went away, and did as the LORD had
commanded Moses and Aaron, so did they.

02:012:029 And it came to pass, that at midnight the LORD smote all the

firstborn in the land of Egypt, from the firstborn of Pharaoh
that sat on his throne unto the firstborn of the captive that
was in the dungeon; and all the firstborn of cattle.

02:012:030 And Pharaoh rose up in the night, he, and all his servants,
and all the Egyptians; and there was a great cry in Egypt; for
there was not a house where there was not one dead.

02:012:031 And he called for Moses and Aaron by night, and said, Rise up,
and get you forth from among my people, both ye and the
children of Israel; and go, serve the LORD, as ye have said.

02:012:032 Also take your flocks and your herds, as ye have said, and be
gone; and bless me also.

02:012:033 And the Egyptians were urgent upon the people, that they might
send them out of the land in haste; for they said, We be all
dead men.

02:012:034 And the people took their dough before it was leavened, their
kneadingtroughs being bound up in their clothes upon their
shoulders.

02:012:035 And the children of Israel did according to the word of Moses;
and they borrowed of the Egyptians jewels of silver, and
jewels of gold, and raiment:

02:012:036 And the LORD gave the people favour in the sight of the
Egyptians, so that they lent unto them such things as they
required. And they spoiled the Egyptians.

02:012:037 And the children of Israel journeyed from Rameses to Succoth,
about six hundred thousand on foot that were men, beside
children.

02:012:038 And a mixed multitude went up also with them; and flocks, and
herds, even very much cattle.

02:012:039 And they baked unleavened cakes of the dough which they

brought forth out of Egypt, for it was not leavened; because
they were thrust out of Egypt, and could not tarry, neither
had they prepared for themselves any victual.

02:012:040 Now the sojourning of the children of Israel, who dwelt in
Egypt, was four hundred and thirty years.

02:012:041 And it came to pass at the end of the four hundred and thirty
years, even the selfsame day it came to pass, that all the
hosts of the LORD went out from the land of Egypt.

02:012:042 It is a night to be much observed unto the LORD for bringing
them out from the land of Egypt: this is that night of the
LORD to be observed of all the children of Israel in their
generations.

02:012:043 And the LORD said unto Moses and Aaron, This is the ordinance
of the passover: There shall no stranger eat thereof:

02:012:044 But every man's servant that is bought for money, when thou
hast circumcised him, then shall he eat thereof.

02:012:045 A foreigner and an hired servant shall not eat thereof.

02:012:046 In one house shall it be eaten; thou shalt not carry forth
ought of the flesh abroad out of the house; neither shall ye
break a bone thereof.

02:012:047 All the congregation of Israel shall keep it.

02:012:048 And when a stranger shall sojourn with thee, and will keep the
passover to the LORD, let all his males be circumcised, and
then let him come near and keep it; and he shall be as one
that is born in the land: for no uncircumcised person shall
eat thereof.

02:012:049 One law shall be to him that is homeborn, and unto the
stranger that sojourneth among you.

02:012:050 Thus did all the children of Israel; as the LORD commanded
Moses and Aaron, so did they.

02:012:051 And it came to pass the selfsame day, that the LORD did bring
the children of Israel out of the land of Egypt by their
armies.

02:013:001 And the LORD spake unto Moses, saying,

02:013:002 Sanctify unto me all the firstborn, whatsoever openeth the
womb among the children of Israel, both of man and of beast:
it is mine.

02:013:003 And Moses said unto the people, Remember this day, in which ye
came out from Egypt, out of the house of bondage; for by
strength of hand the LORD brought you out from this place:
there shall no leavened bread be eaten.

02:013:004 This day came ye out in the month Abib.

02:013:005 And it shall be when the LORD shall bring thee into the land
of the Canaanites, and the Hittites, and the Amorites, and the
Hivites, and the Jebusites, which he sware unto thy fathers to
give thee, a land flowing with milk and honey, that thou shalt
keep this service in this month.

02:013:006 Seven days thou shalt eat unleavened bread, and in the seventh
day shall be a feast to the LORD.

02:013:007 Unleavened bread shall be eaten seven days; and there shall no
leavened bread be seen with thee, neither shall there be
leaven seen with thee in all thy quarters.

02:013:008 And thou shalt shew thy son in that day, saying, This is done
because of that which the LORD did unto me when I came forth
out of Egypt.

02:013:009 And it shall be for a sign unto thee upon thine hand, and for
a memorial between thine eyes, that the LORD's law may be in

thy mouth: for with a strong hand hath the LORD brought thee
out of Egypt.

02:013:010 Thou shalt therefore keep this ordinance in his season from
year to year.

02:013:011 And it shall be when the LORD shall bring thee into the land
of the Canaanites, as he sware unto thee and to thy fathers,
and shall give it thee,

02:013:012 That thou shalt set apart unto the LORD all that openeth the
matrix, and every firstling that cometh of a beast which thou
hast; the males shall be the LORD's.

02:013:013 And every firstling of an ass thou shalt redeem with a lamb;
and if thou wilt not redeem it, then thou shalt break his
neck: and all the firstborn of man among thy children shalt
thou redeem.

02:013:014 And it shall be when thy son asketh thee in time to come,
saying, What is this? that thou shalt say unto him, By
strength of hand the LORD brought us out from Egypt, from the
house of bondage:

02:013:015 And it came to pass, when Pharaoh would hardly let us go, that
the LORD slew all the firstborn in the land of Egypt, both the
firstborn of man, and the firstborn of beast: therefore I
sacrifice to the LORD all that openeth the matrix, being
males; but all the firstborn of my children I redeem.

02:013:016 And it shall be for a token upon thine hand, and for frontlets
between thine eyes: for by strength of hand the LORD brought
us forth out of Egypt.

02:013:017 And it came to pass, when Pharaoh had let the people go, that
God led them not through the way of the land of the
Philistines, although that was near; for God said, Lest
peradventure the people repent when they see war, and they

return to Egypt:

02:013:018 But God led the people about, through the way of the wilderness of the Red sea: and the children of Israel went up harnessed out of the land of Egypt.

02:013:019 And Moses took the bones of Joseph with him: for he had straitly sworn the children of Israel, saying, God will surely visit you; and ye shall carry up my bones away hence with you.

02:013:020 And they took their journey from Succoth, and encamped in Etham, in the edge of the wilderness.

02:013:021 And the LORD went before them by day in a pillar of a cloud, to lead them the way; and by night in a pillar of fire, to give them light; to go by day and night:

02:013:022 He took not away the pillar of the cloud by day, nor the pillar of fire by night, from before the people.

02:014:001 And the LORD spake unto Moses, saying,

02:014:002 Speak unto the children of Israel, that they turn and encamp before Pihahiroth, between Migdol and the sea, over against Baalzephon: before it shall ye encamp by the sea.

02:014:003 For Pharaoh will say of the children of Israel, They are entangled in the land, the wilderness hath shut them in.

02:014:004 And I will harden Pharaoh's heart, that he shall follow after them; and I will be honoured upon Pharaoh, and upon all his host; that the Egyptians may know that I am the LORD. And they did so.

02:014:005 And it was told the king of Egypt that the people fled: and the heart of Pharaoh and of his servants was turned against the people, and they said, Why have we done this, that we have let Israel go from serving us?

02:014:006 And he made ready his chariot, and took his people with him:

02:014:007 And he took six hundred chosen chariots, and all the chariots
of Egypt, and captains over every one of them.

02:014:008 And the LORD hardened the heart of Pharaoh king of Egypt, and
he pursued after the children of Israel: and the children of
Israel went out with an high hand.

02:014:009 But the Egyptians pursued after them, all the horses and
chariots of Pharaoh, and his horsemen, and his army, and
overtook them encamping by the sea, beside Pihahiroth, before
Baalzephon.

02:014:010 And when Pharaoh drew nigh, the children of Israel lifted up
their eyes, and, behold, the Egyptians marched after them; and
they were sore afraid: and the children of Israel cried out
unto the LORD.

02:014:011 And they said unto Moses, Because there were no graves in
Egypt, hast thou taken us away to die in the wilderness?
wherefore hast thou dealt thus with us, to carry us forth out
of Egypt?

02:014:012 Is not this the word that we did tell thee in Egypt, saying,
Let us alone, that we may serve the Egyptians? For it had been
better for us to serve the Egyptians, than that we should die
in the wilderness.

02:014:013 And Moses said unto the people, Fear ye not, stand still, and
see the salvation of the LORD, which he will shew to you to
day: for the Egyptians whom ye have seen to day, ye shall see
them again no more for ever.

02:014:014 The LORD shall fight for you, and ye shall hold your peace.

02:014:015 And the LORD said unto Moses, Wherefore criest thou unto me?
speak unto the children of Israel, that they go forward:

02:014:016 But lift thou up thy rod, and stretch out thine hand over the
sea, and divide it: and the children of Israel shall go on dry
ground through the midst of the sea.

02:014:017 And I, behold, I will harden the hearts of the Egyptians, and
they shall follow them: and I will get me honour upon Pharaoh,
and upon all his host, upon his chariots, and upon his
horsemen.

02:014:018 And the Egyptians shall know that I am the LORD, when I have
gotten me honour upon Pharaoh, upon his chariots, and upon his
horsemen.

02:014:019 And the angel of God, which went before the camp of Israel,
removed and went behind them; and the pillar of the cloud went
from before their face, and stood behind them:

02:014:020 And it came between the camp of the Egyptians and the camp of
Israel; and it was a cloud and darkness to them, but it gave
light by night to these: so that the one came not near the
other all the night.

02:014:021 And Moses stretched out his hand over the sea; and the LORD
caused the sea to go back by a strong east wind all that
night, and made the sea dry land, and the waters were divided.

02:014:022 And the children of Israel went into the midst of the sea upon
the dry ground: and the waters were a wall unto them on their
right hand, and on their left.

02:014:023 And the Egyptians pursued, and went in after them to the midst
of the sea, even all Pharaoh's horses, his chariots, and his
horsemen.

02:014:024 And it came to pass, that in the morning watch the LORD looked
unto the host of the Egyptians through the pillar of fire and
of the cloud, and troubled the host of the Egyptians,

02:014:025 And took off their chariot wheels, that they drave them

heavily: so that the Egyptians said, Let us flee from the face
of Israel; for the LORD fighteth for them against the
Egyptians.

02:014:026 And the LORD said unto Moses, Stretch out thine hand over the
sea, that the waters may come again upon the Egyptians, upon
their chariots, and upon their horsemen.

02:014:027 And Moses stretched forth his hand over the sea, and the sea
returned to his strength when the morning appeared; and the
Egyptians fled against it; and the LORD overthrew the
Egyptians in the midst of the sea.

02:014:028 And the waters returned, and covered the chariots, and the
horsemen, and all the host of Pharaoh that came into the sea
after them; there remained not so much as one of them.

02:014:029 But the children of Israel walked upon dry land in the midst
of the sea; and the waters were a wall unto them on their
right hand, and on their left.

02:014:030 Thus the LORD saved Israel that day out of the hand of the
Egyptians; and Israel saw the Egyptians dead upon the sea
shore.

02:014:031 And Israel saw that great work which the LORD did upon the
Egyptians: and the people feared the LORD, and believed the
LORD, and his servant Moses.

02:015:001 Then sang Moses and the children of Israel this song unto the
LORD, and spake, saying, I will sing unto the LORD, for he
hath triumphed gloriously: the horse and his rider hath he
thrown into the sea.

02:015:002 The LORD is my strength and song, and he is become my
salvation: he is my God, and I will prepare him an habitation;
my father's God, and I will exalt him.

02:015:003 The LORD is a man of war: the LORD is his name.

02:015:004 Pharaoh's chariots and his host hath he cast into the sea: his chosen captains also are drowned in the Red sea.

02:015:005 The depths have covered them: they sank into the bottom as a stone.

02:015:006 Thy right hand, O LORD, is become glorious in power: thy right hand, O LORD, hath dashed in pieces the enemy.

02:015:007 And in the greatness of thine excellency thou hast overthrown them that rose up against thee: thou sentest forth thy wrath, which consumed them as stubble.

02:015:008 And with the blast of thy nostrils the waters were gathered together, the floods stood upright as an heap, and the depths were congealed in the heart of the sea.

02:015:009 The enemy said, I will pursue, I will overtake, I will divide the spoil; my lust shall be satisfied upon them; I will draw my sword, my hand shall destroy them.

02:015:010 Thou didst blow with thy wind, the sea covered them: they sank as lead in the mighty waters.

02:015:011 Who is like unto thee, O LORD, among the gods? who is like thee, glorious in holiness, fearful in praises, doing wonders?

02:015:012 Thou stretchedst out thy right hand, the earth swallowed them.

02:015:013 Thou in thy mercy hast led forth the people which thou hast redeemed: thou hast guided them in thy strength unto thy holy habitation.

02:015:014 The people shall hear, and be afraid: sorrow shall take hold on the inhabitants of Palestina.

02:015:015 Then the dukes of Edom shall be amazed; the mighty men of Moab, trembling shall take hold upon them; all the inhabitants of Canaan shall melt away.

02:015:016 Fear and dread shall fall upon them; by the greatness of thine
arm they shall be as still as a stone; till thy people pass
over, O LORD, till the people pass over, which thou hast
purchased.

02:015:017 Thou shalt bring them in, and plant them in the mountain of
thine inheritance, in the place, O LORD, which thou hast made
for thee to dwell in, in the Sanctuary, O LORD, which thy
hands have established.

02:015:018 The LORD shall reign for ever and ever.

02:015:019 For the horse of Pharaoh went in with his chariots and with
his horsemen into the sea, and the LORD brought again the
waters of the sea upon them; but the children of Israel went
on dry land in the midst of the sea.

02:015:020 And Miriam the prophetess, the sister of Aaron, took a timbrel
in her hand; and all the women went out after her with
timbrels and with dances.

02:015:021 And Miriam answered them, Sing ye to the LORD, for he hath
triumphed gloriously; the horse and his rider hath he thrown
into the sea.

02:015:022 So Moses brought Israel from the Red sea, and they went out
into the wilderness of Shur; and they went three days in the
wilderness, and found no water.

02:015:023 And when they came to Marah, they could not drink of the
waters of Marah, for they were bitter: therefore the name of
it was called Marah.

02:015:024 And the people murmured against Moses, saying, What shall we
drink?

02:015:025 And he cried unto the LORD; and the LORD shewed him a tree,
which when he had cast into the waters, the waters were made
sweet: there he made for them a statute and an ordinance, and

there he proved them,

02:015:026 And said, If thou wilt diligently hearken to the voice of the LORD thy God, and wilt do that which is right in his sight, and wilt give ear to his commandments, and keep all his statutes, I will put none of these diseases upon thee, which I have brought upon the Egyptians: for I am the LORD that healeth thee.

02:015:027 And they came to Elim, where were twelve wells of water, and threescore and ten palm trees: and they encamped there by the waters.

02:016:001 And they took their journey from Elim, and all the congregation of the children of Israel came unto the wilderness of Sin, which is between Elim and Sinai, on the fifteenth day of the second month after their departing out of the land of Egypt.

02:016:002 And the whole congregation of the children of Israel murmured against Moses and Aaron in the wilderness:

02:016:003 And the children of Israel said unto them, Would to God we had died by the hand of the LORD in the land of Egypt, when we sat by the flesh pots, and when we did eat bread to the full; for ye have brought us forth into this wilderness, to kill this whole assembly with hunger.

02:016:004 Then said the LORD unto Moses, Behold, I will rain bread from heaven for you; and the people shall go out and gather a certain rate every day, that I may prove them, whether they will walk in my law, or no.

02:016:005 And it shall come to pass, that on the sixth day they shall prepare that which they bring in; and it shall be twice as much as they gather daily.

02:016:006 And Moses and Aaron said unto all the children of Israel, At

even, then ye shall know that the LORD hath brought you out
from the land of Egypt:

02:016:007 And in the morning, then ye shall see the glory of the LORD;
for that he heareth your murmurings against the LORD: and what
are we, that ye murmur against us?

02:016:008 And Moses said, This shall be, when the LORD shall give you in
the evening flesh to eat, and in the morning bread to the
full; for that the LORD heareth your murmurings which ye
murmur against him: and what are we? your murmurings are not
against us, but against the LORD.

02:016:009 And Moses spake unto Aaron, Say unto all the congregation of
the children of Israel, Come near before the LORD: for he hath
heard your murmurings.

02:016:010 And it came to pass, as Aaron spake unto the whole
congregation of the children of Israel, that they looked
toward the wilderness, and, behold, the glory of the LORD
appeared in the cloud.

02:016:011 And the LORD spake unto Moses, saying,

02:016:012 I have heard the murmurings of the children of Israel: speak
unto them, saying, At even ye shall eat flesh, and in the
morning ye shall be filled with bread; and ye shall know that
I am the LORD your God.

02:016:013 And it came to pass, that at even the quails came up, and
covered the camp: and in the morning the dew lay round about
the host.

02:016:014 And when the dew that lay was gone up, behold, upon the face
of the wilderness there lay a small round thing, as small as
the hoar frost on the ground.

02:016:015 And when the children of Israel saw it, they said one to
another, It is manna: for they wist not what it was. And Moses

said unto them, This is the bread which the LORD hath given
you to eat.

02:016:016 This is the thing which the LORD hath commanded, Gather of it
every man according to his eating, an omer for every man,
according to the number of your persons; take ye every man for
them which are in his tents.

02:016:017 And the children of Israel did so, and gathered, some more,
some less.

02:016:018 And when they did mete it with an omer, he that gathered much
had nothing over, and he that gathered little had no lack;
they gathered every man according to his eating.

02:016:019 And Moses said, Let no man leave of it till the morning.

02:016:020 Notwithstanding they hearkened not unto Moses; but some of
them left of it until the morning, and it bred worms, and
stank: and Moses was wroth with them.

02:016:021 And they gathered it every morning, every man according to his
eating: and when the sun waxed hot, it melted.

02:016:022 And it came to pass, that on the sixth day they gathered twice
as much bread, two omers for one man: and all the rulers of
the congregation came and told Moses.

02:016:023 And he said unto them, This is that which the LORD hath said,
To morrow is the rest of the holy sabbath unto the LORD: bake
that which ye will bake to day, and seethe that ye will
seethe; and that which remaineth over lay up for you to be
kept until the morning.

02:016:024 And they laid it up till the morning, as Moses bade: and it
did not stink, neither was there any worm therein.

02:016:025 And Moses said, Eat that to day; for to day is a sabbath unto
the LORD: to day ye shall not find it in the field.

02:016:026 Six days ye shall gather it; but on the seventh day, which is the sabbath, in it there shall be none.

02:016:027 And it came to pass, that there went out some of the people on the seventh day for to gather, and they found none.

02:016:028 And the LORD said unto Moses, How long refuse ye to keep my commandments and my laws?

02:016:029 See, for that the LORD hath given you the sabbath, therefore he giveth you on the sixth day the bread of two days; abide ye every man in his place, let no man go out of his place on the seventh day.

02:016:030 So the people rested on the seventh day.

02:016:031 And the house of Israel called the name thereof Manna: and it was like coriander seed, white; and the taste of it was like wafers made with honey.

02:016:032 And Moses said, This is the thing which the LORD commandeth, Fill an omer of it to be kept for your generations; that they may see the bread wherewith I have fed you in the wilderness, when I brought you forth from the land of Egypt.

02:016:033 And Moses said unto Aaron, Take a pot, and put an omer full of manna therein, and lay it up before the LORD, to be kept for your generations.

02:016:034 As the LORD commanded Moses, so Aaron laid it up before the Testimony, to be kept.

02:016:035 And the children of Israel did eat manna forty years, until they came to a land inhabited; they did eat manna, until they came unto the borders of the land of Canaan.

02:016:036 Now an omer is the tenth part of an ephah.

02:017:001 And all the congregation of the children of Israel journeyed

from the wilderness of Sin, after their journeys, according to
the commandment of the LORD, and pitched in Rephidim: and
there was no water for the people to drink.

02:017:002 Wherefore the people did chide with Moses, and said, Give us
water that we may drink. And Moses said unto them, Why chide
ye with me? wherefore do ye tempt the LORD?

02:017:003 And the people thirsted there for water; and the people
murmured against Moses, and said, Wherefore is this that thou
hast brought us up out of Egypt, to kill us and our children
and our cattle with thirst?

02:017:004 And Moses cried unto the LORD, saying, What shall I do unto
this people? they be almost ready to stone me.

02:017:005 And the LORD said unto Moses, Go on before the people, and
take with thee of the elders of Israel; and thy rod, wherewith
thou smotest the river, take in thine hand, and go.

02:017:006 Behold, I will stand before thee there upon the rock in Horeb;
and thou shalt smite the rock, and there shall come water out
of it, that the people may drink. And Moses did so in the
sight of the elders of Israel.

02:017:007 And he called the name of the place Massah, and Meribah,
because of the chiding of the children of Israel, and because
they tempted the LORD, saying, Is the LORD among us, or not?

02:017:008 Then came Amalek, and fought with Israel in Rephidim.

02:017:009 And Moses said unto Joshua, Choose us out men, and go out,
fight with Amalek: to morrow I will stand on the top of the
hill with the rod of God in mine hand.

02:017:010 So Joshua did as Moses had said to him, and fought with
Amalek: and Moses, Aaron, and Hur went up to the top of the
hill.

02:017:011 And it came to pass, when Moses held up his hand, that Israel prevailed: and when he let down his hand, Amalek prevailed.

02:017:012 But Moses hands were heavy; and they took a stone, and put it under him, and he sat thereon; and Aaron and Hur stayed up his hands, the one on the one side, and the other on the other side; and his hands were steady until the going down of the sun.

02:017:013 And Joshua discomfited Amalek and his people with the edge of the sword.

02:017:014 And the LORD said unto Moses, Write this for a memorial in a book, and rehearse it in the ears of Joshua: for I will utterly put out the remembrance of Amalek from under heaven.

02:017:015 And Moses built an altar, and called the name of it Jehovahnissi:

02:017:016 For he said, Because the LORD hath sworn that the LORD will have war with Amalek from generation to generation.

02:018:001 When Jethro, the priest of Midian, Moses' father in law, heard of all that God had done for Moses, and for Israel his people, and that the LORD had brought Israel out of Egypt;

02:018:002 Then Jethro, Moses' father in law, took Zipporah, Moses' wife, after he had sent her back,

02:018:003 And her two sons; of which the name of the one was Gershom; for he said, I have been an alien in a strange land:

02:018:004 And the name of the other was Eliezer; for the God of my father, said he, was mine help, and delivered me from the sword of Pharaoh:

02:018:005 And Jethro, Moses' father in law, came with his sons and his wife unto Moses into the wilderness, where he encamped at the mount of God:

02:018:006 And he said unto Moses, I thy father in law Jethro am come
unto thee, and thy wife, and her two sons with her.

02:018:007 And Moses went out to meet his father in law, and did
obeisance, and kissed him; and they asked each other of their
welfare; and they came into the tent.

02:018:008 And Moses told his father in law all that the LORD had done
unto Pharaoh and to the Egyptians for Israel's sake, and all
the travail that had come upon them by the way, and how the
LORD delivered them.

02:018:009 And Jethro rejoiced for all the goodness which the LORD had
done to Israel, whom he had delivered out of the hand of the
Egyptians.

02:018:010 And Jethro said, Blessed be the LORD, who hath delivered you
out of the hand of the Egyptians, and out of the hand of
Pharaoh, who hath delivered the people from under the hand of
the Egyptians.

02:018:011 Now I know that the LORD is greater than all gods: for in the
thing wherein they dealt proudly he was above them.

02:018:012 And Jethro, Moses' father in law, took a burnt offering and
sacrifices for God: and Aaron came, and all the elders of
Israel, to eat bread with Moses' father in law before God.

02:018:013 And it came to pass on the morrow, that Moses sat to judge the
people: and the people stood by Moses from the morning unto
the evening.

02:018:014 And when Moses' father in law saw all that he did to the
people, he said, What is this thing that thou doest to the
people? why sittest thou thyself alone, and all the people
stand by thee from morning unto even?

02:018:015 And Moses said unto his father in law, Because the people come
unto me to enquire of God:

02:018:016 When they have a matter, they come unto me; and I judge
between one and another, and I do make them know the statutes
of God, and his laws.

02:018:017 And Moses' father in law said unto him, The thing that thou
doest is not good.

02:018:018 Thou wilt surely wear away, both thou, and this people that is
with thee: for this thing is too heavy for thee; thou art not
able to perform it thyself alone.

02:018:019 Hearken now unto my voice, I will give thee counsel, and God
shall be with thee: Be thou for the people to God-ward, that
thou mayest bring the causes unto God:

02:018:020 And thou shalt teach them ordinances and laws, and shalt shew
them the way wherein they must walk, and the work that they
must do.

02:018:021 Moreover thou shalt provide out of all the people able men,
such as fear God, men of truth, hating covetousness; and place
such over them, to be rulers of thousands, and rulers of
hundreds, rulers of fifties, and rulers of tens:

02:018:022 And let them judge the people at all seasons: and it shall be,
that every great matter they shall bring unto thee, but every
small matter they shall judge: so shall it be easier for
thyself, and they shall bear the burden with thee.

02:018:023 If thou shalt do this thing, and God command thee so, then
thou shalt be able to endure, and all this people shall also
go to their place in peace.

02:018:024 So Moses hearkened to the voice of his father in law, and did
all that he had said.

02:018:025 And Moses chose able men out of all Israel, and made them
heads over the people, rulers of thousands, rulers of
hundreds, rulers of fifties, and rulers of tens.

02:018:026 And they judged the people at all seasons: the hard causes
they brought unto Moses, but every small matter they judged
themselves.

02:018:027 And Moses let his father in law depart; and he went his way
into his own land.

02:019:001 In the third month, when the children of Israel were gone
forth out of the land of Egypt, the same day came they into
the wilderness of Sinai.

02:019:002 For they were departed from Rephidim, and were come to the
desert of Sinai, and had pitched in the wilderness; and there
Israel camped before the mount.

02:019:003 And Moses went up unto God, and the LORD called unto him out
of the mountain, saying, Thus shalt thou say to the house of
Jacob, and tell the children of Israel;

02:019:004 Ye have seen what I did unto the Egyptians, and how I bare you
on eagles' wings, and brought you unto myself.

02:019:005 Now therefore, if ye will obey my voice indeed, and keep my
covenant, then ye shall be a peculiar treasure unto me above
all people: for all the earth is mine:

02:019:006 And ye shall be unto me a kingdom of priests, and an holy
nation. These are the words which thou shalt speak unto the
children of Israel.

02:019:007 And Moses came and called for the elders of the people, and
laid before their faces all these words which the LORD
commanded him.

02:019:008 And all the people answered together, and said, All that the
LORD hath spoken we will do. And Moses returned the words of
the people unto the LORD.

02:019:009 And the LORD said unto Moses, Lo, I come unto thee in a thick

cloud, that the people may hear when I speak with thee, and
believe thee for ever. And Moses told the words of the people
unto the LORD.

02:019:010 And the LORD said unto Moses, Go unto the people, and sanctify
them to day and to morrow, and let them wash their clothes,

02:019:011 And be ready against the third day: for the third day the LORD
will come down in the sight of all the people upon mount
Sinai.

02:019:012 And thou shalt set bounds unto the people round about, saying,
Take heed to yourselves, that ye go not up into the mount, or
touch the border of it: whosoever toucheth the mount shall be
surely put to death:

02:019:013 There shall not an hand touch it, but he shall surely be
stoned, or shot through; whether it be beast or man, it shall
not live: when the trumpet soundeth long, they shall come up
to the mount.

02:019:014 And Moses went down from the mount unto the people, and
sanctified the people; and they washed their clothes.

02:019:015 And he said unto the people, Be ready against the third day:
come not at your wives.

02:019:016 And it came to pass on the third day in the morning, that
there were thunders and lightnings, and a thick cloud upon the
mount, and the voice of the trumpet exceeding loud; so that
all the people that was in the camp trembled.

02:019:017 And Moses brought forth the people out of the camp to meet
with God; and they stood at the nether part of the mount.

02:019:018 And mount Sinai was altogether on a smoke, because the LORD
descended upon it in fire: and the smoke thereof ascended as
the smoke of a furnace, and the whole mount quaked greatly.

02:019:019 And when the voice of the trumpet sounded long, and waxed louder and louder, Moses spake, and God answered him by a voice.

02:019:020 And the LORD came down upon mount Sinai, on the top of the mount: and the LORD called Moses up to the top of the mount; and Moses went up.

02:019:021 And the LORD said unto Moses, Go down, charge the people, lest they break through unto the LORD to gaze, and many of them perish.

02:019:022 And let the priests also, which come near to the LORD, sanctify themselves, lest the LORD break forth upon them.

02:019:023 And Moses said unto the LORD, The people cannot come up to mount Sinai: for thou chargedst us, saying, Set bounds about the mount, and sanctify it.

02:019:024 And the LORD said unto him, Away, get thee down, and thou shalt come up, thou, and Aaron with thee: but let not the priests and the people break through to come up unto the LORD, lest he break forth upon them.

02:019:025 So Moses went down unto the people, and spake unto them.

02:020:001 And God spake all these words, saying,

02:020:002 I am the LORD thy God, which have brought thee out of the land of Egypt, out of the house of bondage.

02:020:003 Thou shalt have no other gods before me.

02:020:004 Thou shalt not make unto thee any graven image, or any likeness of any thing that is in heaven above, or that is in the earth beneath, or that is in the water under the earth.

02:020:005 Thou shalt not bow down thyself to them, nor serve them: for I the LORD thy God am a jealous God, visiting the iniquity of

the fathers upon the children unto the third and fourth
generation of them that hate me;

02:020:006 And shewing mercy unto thousands of them that love me, and
keep my commandments.

02:020:007 Thou shalt not take the name of the LORD thy God in vain; for
the LORD will not hold him guiltless that taketh his name in
vain.

02:020:008 Remember the sabbath day, to keep it holy.

02:020:009 Six days shalt thou labour, and do all thy work:

02:020:010 But the seventh day is the sabbath of the LORD thy God: in it
thou shalt not do any work, thou, nor thy son, nor thy
daughter, thy manservant, nor thy maidservant, nor thy cattle,
nor thy stranger that is within thy gates:

02:020:011 For in six days the LORD made heaven and earth, the sea, and
all that in them is, and rested the seventh day: wherefore the
LORD blessed the sabbath day, and hallowed it.

02:020:012 Honour thy father and thy mother: that thy days may be long
upon the land which the LORD thy God giveth thee.

02:020:013 Thou shalt not kill.

02:020:014 Thou shalt not commit adultery.

02:020:015 Thou shalt not steal.

02:020:016 Thou shalt not bear false witness against thy neighbour.

02:020:017 Thou shalt not covet thy neighbour's house, thou shalt not
covet thy neighbour's wife, nor his manservant, nor his
maidservant, nor his ox, nor his ass, nor any thing that is
thy neighbour's.

02:020:018 And all the people saw the thunderings, and the lightnings,

and the noise of the trumpet, and the mountain smoking: and
when the people saw it, they removed, and stood afar off.

02:020:019 And they said unto Moses, Speak thou with us, and we will hear: but let not God speak with us, lest we die.

02:020:020 And Moses said unto the people, Fear not: for God is come to prove you, and that his fear may be before your faces, that ye sin not.

02:020:021 And the people stood afar off, and Moses drew near unto the thick darkness where God was.

02:020:022 And the LORD said unto Moses, Thus thou shalt say unto the children of Israel, Ye have seen that I have talked with you from heaven.

02:020:023 Ye shall not make with me gods of silver, neither shall ye make unto you gods of gold.

02:020:024 An altar of earth thou shalt make unto me, and shalt sacrifice thereon thy burnt offerings, and thy peace offerings, thy sheep, and thine oxen: in all places where I record my name I will come unto thee, and I will bless thee.

02:020:025 And if thou wilt make me an altar of stone, thou shalt not build it of hewn stone: for if thou lift up thy tool upon it, thou hast polluted it.

02:020:026 Neither shalt thou go up by steps unto mine altar, that thy nakedness be not discovered thereon.

02:021:001 Now these are the judgments which thou shalt set before them.

02:021:002 If thou buy an Hebrew servant, six years he shall serve: and in the seventh he shall go out free for nothing.

02:021:003 If he came in by himself, he shall go out by himself: if he were married, then his wife shall go out with him.

02:021:004 If his master have given him a wife, and she have born him
sons or daughters; the wife and her children shall be her
master's, and he shall go out by himself.

02:021:005 And if the servant shall plainly say, I love my master, my
wife, and my children; I will not go out free:

02:021:006 Then his master shall bring him unto the judges; he shall also
bring him to the door, or unto the door post; and his master
shall bore his ear through with an aul; and he shall serve him
for ever.

02:021:007 And if a man sell his daughter to be a maidservant, she shall
not go out as the menservants do.

02:021:008 If she please not her master, who hath betrothed her to
himself, then shall he let her be redeemed: to sell her unto a
strange nation he shall have no power, seeing he hath dealt
deceitfully with her.

02:021:009 And if he have betrothed her unto his son, he shall deal with
her after the manner of daughters.

02:021:010 If he take him another wife; her food, her raiment, and her
duty of marriage, shall he not diminish.

02:021:011 And if he do not these three unto her, then shall she go out
free without money.

02:021:012 He that smiteth a man, so that he die, shall be surely put to
death.

02:021:013 And if a man lie not in wait, but God deliver him into his
hand; then I will appoint thee a place whither he shall flee.

02:021:014 But if a man come presumptuously upon his neighbour, to slay
him with guile; thou shalt take him from mine altar, that he
may die.

02:021:015 And he that smiteth his father, or his mother, shall be surely put to death.

02:021:016 And he that stealeth a man, and selleth him, or if he be found in his hand, he shall surely be put to death.

02:021:017 And he that curseth his father, or his mother, shall surely be put to death.

02:021:018 And if men strive together, and one smite another with a stone, or with his fist, and he die not, but keepeth his bed:

02:021:019 If he rise again, and walk abroad upon his staff, then shall he that smote him be quit: only he shall pay for the loss of his time, and shall cause him to be thoroughly healed.

02:021:020 And if a man smite his servant, or his maid, with a rod, and he die under his hand; he shall be surely punished.

02:021:021 Notwithstanding, if he continue a day or two, he shall not be punished: for he is his money.

02:021:022 If men strive, and hurt a woman with child, so that her fruit depart from her, and yet no mischief follow: he shall be surely punished, according as the woman's husband will lay upon him; and he shall pay as the judges determine.

02:021:023 And if any mischief follow, then thou shalt give life for life,

02:021:024 Eye for eye, tooth for tooth, hand for hand, foot for foot,

02:021:025 Burning for burning, wound for wound, stripe for stripe.

02:021:026 And if a man smite the eye of his servant, or the eye of his maid, that it perish; he shall let him go free for his eye's sake.

02:021:027 And if he smite out his manservant's tooth, or his

maidservant's tooth; he shall let him go free for his tooth's
sake.

02:021:028 If an ox gore a man or a woman, that they die: then the ox
shall be surely stoned, and his flesh shall not be eaten; but
the owner of the ox shall be quit.

02:021:029 But if the ox were wont to push with his horn in time past,
and it hath been testified to his owner, and he hath not kept
him in, but that he hath killed a man or a woman; the ox shall
be stoned, and his owner also shall be put to death.

02:021:030 If there be laid on him a sum of money, then he shall give for
the ransom of his life whatsoever is laid upon him.

02:021:031 Whether he have gored a son, or have gored a daughter,
according to this judgment shall it be done unto him.

02:021:032 If the ox shall push a manservant or a maidservant; he shall
give unto their master thirty shekels of silver, and the ox
shall be stoned.

02:021:033 And if a man shall open a pit, or if a man shall dig a pit,
and not cover it, and an ox or an ass fall therein;

02:021:034 The owner of the pit shall make it good, and give money unto
the owner of them; and the dead beast shall be his.

02:021:035 And if one man's ox hurt another's, that he die; then they
shall sell the live ox, and divide the money of it; and the
dead ox also they shall divide.

02:021:036 Or if it be known that the ox hath used to push in time past,
and his owner hath not kept him in; he shall surely pay ox for
ox; and the dead shall be his own.

02:022:001 If a man shall steal an ox, or a sheep, and kill it, or sell
it; he shall restore five oxen for an ox, and four sheep for a
sheep.

02:022:002 If a thief be found breaking up, and be smitten that he die, there shall no blood be shed for him.

02:022:003 If the sun be risen upon him, there shall be blood shed for him; for he should make full restitution; if he have nothing, then he shall be sold for his theft.

02:022:004 If the theft be certainly found in his hand alive, whether it be ox, or ass, or sheep; he shall restore double.

02:022:005 If a man shall cause a field or vineyard to be eaten, and shall put in his beast, and shall feed in another man's field; of the best of his own field, and of the best of his own vineyard, shall he make restitution.

02:022:006 If fire break out, and catch in thorns, so that the stacks of corn, or the standing corn, or the field, be consumed therewith; he that kindled the fire shall surely make restitution.

02:022:007 If a man shall deliver unto his neighbour money or stuff to keep, and it be stolen out of the man's house; if the thief be found, let him pay double.

02:022:008 If the thief be not found, then the master of the house shall be brought unto the judges, to see whether he have put his hand unto his neighbour's goods.

02:022:009 For all manner of trespass, whether it be for ox, for ass, for sheep, for raiment, or for any manner of lost thing which another challengeth to be his, the cause of both parties shall come before the judges; and whom the judges shall condemn, he shall pay double unto his neighbour.

02:022:010 If a man deliver unto his neighbour an ass, or an ox, or a sheep, or any beast, to keep; and it die, or be hurt, or driven away, no man seeing it:

02:022:011 Then shall an oath of the LORD be between them both, that he

hath not put his hand unto his neighbour's goods; and the
owner of it shall accept thereof, and he shall not make it
good.

02:022:012 And if it be stolen from him, he shall make restitution unto
the owner thereof.

02:022:013 If it be torn in pieces, then let him bring it for witness,
and he shall not make good that which was torn.

02:022:014 And if a man borrow ought of his neighbour, and it be hurt, or
die, the owner thereof being not with it, he shall surely make
it good.

02:022:015 But if the owner thereof be with it, he shall not make it
good: if it be an hired thing, it came for his hire.

02:022:016 And if a man entice a maid that is not betrothed, and lie with
her, he shall surely endow her to be his wife.

02:022:017 If her father utterly refuse to give her unto him, he shall
pay money according to the dowry of virgins.

02:022:018 Thou shalt not suffer a witch to live.

02:022:019 Whosoever lieth with a beast shall surely be put to death.

02:022:020 He that sacrificeth unto any god, save unto the LORD only, he
shall be utterly destroyed.

02:022:021 Thou shalt neither vex a stranger, nor oppress him: for ye
were strangers in the land of Egypt.

02:022:022 Ye shall not afflict any widow, or fatherless child.

02:022:023 If thou afflict them in any wise, and they cry at all unto me,
I will surely hear their cry;

02:022:024 And my wrath shall wax hot, and I will kill you with the
sword; and your wives shall be widows, and your children

fatherless.

02:022:025 If thou lend money to any of my people that is poor by thee,
thou shalt not be to him as an usurer, neither shalt thou lay
upon him usury.

02:022:026 If thou at all take thy neighbour's raiment to pledge, thou
shalt deliver it unto him by that the sun goeth down:

02:022:027 For that is his covering only, it is his raiment for his skin:
wherein shall he sleep? and it shall come to pass, when he
crieth unto me, that I will hear; for I am gracious.

02:022:028 Thou shalt not revile the gods, nor curse the ruler of thy
people.

02:022:029 Thou shalt not delay to offer the first of thy ripe fruits,
and of thy liquors: the firstborn of thy sons shalt thou give
unto me.

02:022:030 Likewise shalt thou do with thine oxen, and with thy sheep:
seven days it shall be with his dam; on the eighth day thou
shalt give it me.

02:022:031 And ye shall be holy men unto me: neither shall ye eat any
flesh that is torn of beasts in the field; ye shall cast it to
the dogs.

02:023:001 Thou shalt not raise a false report: put not thine hand with
the wicked to be an unrighteous witness.

02:023:002 Thou shalt not follow a multitude to do evil; neither shalt
thou speak in a cause to decline after many to wrest judgment:

02:023:003 Neither shalt thou countenance a poor man in his cause.

02:023:004 If thou meet thine enemy's ox or his ass going astray, thou
shalt surely bring it back to him again.

02:023:005 If thou see the ass of him that hateth thee lying under his
burden, and wouldest forbear to help him, thou shalt surely
help with him.

02:023:006 Thou shalt not wrest the judgment of thy poor in his cause.

02:023:007 Keep thee far from a false matter; and the innocent and
righteous slay thou not: for I will not justify the wicked.

02:023:008 And thou shalt take no gift: for the gift blindeth the wise,
and perverteth the words of the righteous.

02:023:009 Also thou shalt not oppress a stranger: for ye know the heart
of a stranger, seeing ye were strangers in the land of Egypt.

02:023:010 And six years thou shalt sow thy land, and shalt gather in the
fruits thereof:

02:023:011 But the seventh year thou shalt let it rest and lie still;
that the poor of thy people may eat: and what they leave the
beasts of the field shall eat. In like manner thou shalt deal
with thy vineyard, and with thy oliveyard.

02:023:012 Six days thou shalt do thy work, and on the seventh day thou
shalt rest: that thine ox and thine ass may rest, and the son
of thy handmaid, and the stranger, may be refreshed.

02:023:013 And in all things that I have said unto you be circumspect:
and make no mention of the name of other gods, neither let it
be heard out of thy mouth.

02:023:014 Three times thou shalt keep a feast unto me in the year.

02:023:015 Thou shalt keep the feast of unleavened bread: (thou shalt eat
unleavened bread seven days, as I commanded thee, in the time
appointed of the month Abib; for in it thou camest out from
Egypt: and none shall appear before me empty:)

02:023:016 And the feast of harvest, the firstfruits of thy labours,

which thou hast sown in the field: and the feast of
ingathering, which is in the end of the year, when thou hast
gathered in thy labours out of the field.

02:023:017 Three items in the year all thy males shall appear before the
LORD God.

02:023:018 Thou shalt not offer the blood of my sacrifice with leavened
bread; neither shall the fat of my sacrifice remain until the
morning.

02:023:019 The first of the firstfruits of thy land thou shalt bring into
the house of the LORD thy God. Thou shalt not seethe a kid in
his mother's milk.

02:023:020 Behold, I send an Angel before thee, to keep thee in the way,
and to bring thee into the place which I have prepared.

02:023:021 Beware of him, and obey his voice, provoke him not; for he
will not pardon your transgressions: for my name is in him.

02:023:022 But if thou shalt indeed obey his voice, and do all that I
speak; then I will be an enemy unto thine enemies, and an
adversary unto thine adversaries.

02:023:023 For mine Angel shall go before thee, and bring thee in unto
the Amorites, and the Hittites, and the Perizzites, and the
Canaanites, the Hivites, and the Jebusites: and I will cut
them off.

02:023:024 Thou shalt not bow down to their gods, nor serve them, nor do
after their works: but thou shalt utterly overthrow them, and
quite break down their images.

02:023:025 And ye shall serve the LORD your God, and he shall bless thy
bread, and thy water; and I will take sickness away from the
midst of thee.

02:023:026 There shall nothing cast their young, nor be barren, in thy land: the number of thy days I will fulfil.

02:023:027 I will send my fear before thee, and will destroy all the
people to whom thou shalt come, and I will make all thine
enemies turn their backs unto thee.

02:023:028 And I will send hornets before thee, which shall drive out the
Hivite, the Canaanite, and the Hittite, from before thee.

02:023:029 I will not drive them out from before thee in one year; lest
the land become desolate, and the beast of the field multiply
against thee.

02:023:030 By little and little I will drive them out from before thee,
until thou be increased, and inherit the land.

02:023:031 And I will set thy bounds from the Red sea even unto the sea
of the Philistines, and from the desert unto the river: for I
will deliver the inhabitants of the land into your hand; and
thou shalt drive them out before thee.

02:023:032 Thou shalt make no covenant with them, nor with their gods.

02:023:033 They shall not dwell in thy land, lest they make thee sin
against me: for if thou serve their gods, it will surely be a
snare unto thee.

02:024:001 And he said unto Moses, Come up unto the LORD, thou, and
Aaron, Nadab, and Abihu, and seventy of the elders of Israel;
and worship ye afar off.

02:024:002 And Moses alone shall come near the LORD: but they shall not
come nigh; neither shall the people go up with him.

02:024:003 And Moses came and told the people all the words of the LORD,
and all the judgments: and all the people answered with one
voice, and said, All the words which the LORD hath said will
we do.

02:024:004 And Moses wrote all the words of the LORD, and rose up early
in the morning, and builded an altar under the hill, and
twelve pillars, according to the twelve tribes of Israel.

02:024:005 And he sent young men of the children of Israel, which offered
burnt offerings, and sacrificed peace offerings of oxen unto
the LORD.

02:024:006 And Moses took half of the blood, and put it in basons; and
half of the blood he sprinkled on the altar.

02:024:007 And he took the book of the covenant, and read in the audience
of the people: and they said, All that the LORD hath said will
we do, and be obedient.

02:024:008 And Moses took the blood, and sprinkled it on the people, and
said, Behold the blood of the covenant, which the LORD hath
made with you concerning all these words.

02:024:009 Then went up Moses, and Aaron, Nadab, and Abihu, and seventy
of the elders of Israel:

02:024:010 And they saw the God of Israel: and there was under his feet
as it were a paved work of a sapphire stone, and as it were
the body of heaven in his clearness.

02:024:011 And upon the nobles of the children of Israel he laid not his
hand: also they saw God, and did eat and drink.

02:024:012 And the LORD said unto Moses, Come up to me into the mount,
and be there: and I will give thee tables of stone, and a law,
and commandments which I have written; that thou mayest teach
them.

02:024:013 And Moses rose up, and his minister Joshua: and Moses went up
into the mount of God.

02:024:014 And he said unto the elders, Tarry ye here for us, until we
come again unto you: and, behold, Aaron and Hur are with you:

if any man have any matters to do, let him come unto them.

02:024:015 And Moses went up into the mount, and a cloud covered the mount.

02:024:016 And the glory of the LORD abode upon mount Sinai, and the cloud covered it six days: and the seventh day he called unto Moses out of the midst of the cloud.

02:024:017 And the sight of the glory of the LORD was like devouring fire on the top of the mount in the eyes of the children of Israel.

02:024:018 And Moses went into the midst of the cloud, and gat him up into the mount: and Moses was in the mount forty days and forty nights.

02:025:001 And the LORD spake unto Moses, saying,

02:025:002 Speak unto the children of Israel, that they bring me an offering: of every man that giveth it willingly with his heart ye shall take my offering.

02:025:003 And this is the offering which ye shall take of them; gold, and silver, and brass,

02:025:004 And blue, and purple, and scarlet, and fine linen, and goats' hair,

02:025:005 And rams' skins dyed red, and badgers' skins, and shittim wood,

02:025:006 Oil for the light, spices for anointing oil, and for sweet incense,

02:025:007 Onyx stones, and stones to be set in the ephod, and in the breastplate.

02:025:008 And let them make me a sanctuary; that I may dwell among them.

02:025:009 According to all that I shew thee, after the pattern of the

tabernacle, and the pattern of all the instruments thereof,
even so shall ye make it.

02:025:010 And they shall make an ark of shittim wood: two cubits and a
half shall be the length thereof, and a cubit and a half the
breadth thereof, and a cubit and a half the height thereof.

02:025:011 And thou shalt overlay it with pure gold, within and without
shalt thou overlay it, and shalt make upon it a crown of gold
round about.

02:025:012 And thou shalt cast four rings of gold for it, and put them in
the four corners thereof; and two rings shall be in the one
side of it, and two rings in the other side of it.

02:025:013 And thou shalt make staves of shittim wood, and overlay them
with gold.

02:025:014 And thou shalt put the staves into the rings by the sides of
the ark, that the ark may be borne with them.

02:025:015 The staves shall be in the rings of the ark: they shall not be
taken from it.

02:025:016 And thou shalt put into the ark the testimony which I shall
give thee.

02:025:017 And thou shalt make a mercy seat of pure gold: two cubits and
a half shall be the length thereof, and a cubit and a half the
breadth thereof.

02:025:018 And thou shalt make two cherubims of gold, of beaten work
shalt thou make them, in the two ends of the mercy seat.

02:025:019 And make one cherub on the one end, and the other cherub on
the other end: even of the mercy seat shall ye make the
cherubims on the two ends thereof.

02:025:020 And the cherubims shall stretch forth their wings on high,

covering the mercy seat with their wings, and their faces
shall look one to another; toward the mercy seat shall the
faces of the cherubims be.

02:025:021 And thou shalt put the mercy seat above upon the ark; and in
the ark thou shalt put the testimony that I shall give thee.

02:025:022 And there I will meet with thee, and I will commune with thee
from above the mercy seat, from between the two cherubims
which are upon the ark of the testimony, of all things which I
will give thee in commandment unto the children of Israel.

02:025:023 Thou shalt also make a table of shittim wood: two cubits shall
be the length thereof, and a cubit the breadth thereof, and a
cubit and a half the height thereof.

02:025:024 And thou shalt overlay it with pure gold, and make thereto a
crown of gold round about.

02:025:025 And thou shalt make unto it a border of an hand breadth round
about, and thou shalt make a golden crown to the border
thereof round about.

02:025:026 And thou shalt make for it four rings of gold, and put the
rings in the four corners that are on the four feet thereof.

02:025:027 Over against the border shall the rings be for places of the
staves to bear the table.

02:025:028 And thou shalt make the staves of shittim wood, and overlay
them with gold, that the table may be borne with them.

02:025:029 And thou shalt make the dishes thereof, and spoons thereof,
and covers thereof, and bowls thereof, to cover withal: of
pure gold shalt thou make them.

02:025:030 And thou shalt set upon the table shewbread before me alway.

02:025:031 And thou shalt make a candlestick of pure gold: of beaten work

shall the candlestick be made: his shaft, and his branches,
his bowls, his knops, and his flowers, shall be of the same.

02:025:032 And six branches shall come out of the sides of it; three
branches of the candlestick out of the one side, and three
branches of the candlestick out of the other side:

02:025:033 Three bowls made like unto almonds, with a knop and a flower
in one branch; and three bowls made like almonds in the other
branch, with a knop and a flower: so in the six branches that
come out of the candlestick.

02:025:034 And in the candlesticks shall be four bowls made like unto
almonds, with their knops and their flowers.

02:025:035 And there shall be a knop under two branches of the same, and
a knop under two branches of the same, and a knop under two
branches of the same, according to the six branches that
proceed out of the candlestick.

02:025:036 Their knops and their branches shall be of the same: all it
shall be one beaten work of pure gold.

02:025:037 And thou shalt make the seven lamps thereof: and they shall
light the lamps thereof, that they may give light over against
it.

02:025:038 And the tongs thereof, and the snuffdishes thereof, shall be
of pure gold.

02:025:039 Of a talent of pure gold shall he make it, with all these
vessels.

02:025:040 And look that thou make them after their pattern, which was
shewed thee in the mount.

02:026:001 Moreover thou shalt make the tabernacle with ten curtains of
fine twined linen, and blue, and purple, and scarlet: with
cherubims of cunning work shalt thou make them.

02:026:002 The length of one curtain shall be eight and twenty cubits,
and the breadth of one curtain four cubits: and every one of
the curtains shall have one measure.

02:026:003 The five curtains shall be coupled together one to another;
and other five curtains shall be coupled one to another.

02:026:004 And thou shalt make loops of blue upon the edge of the one
curtain from the selvedge in the coupling; and likewise shalt
thou make in the uttermost edge of another curtain, in the
coupling of the second.

02:026:005 Fifty loops shalt thou make in the one curtain, and fifty
loops shalt thou make in the edge of the curtain that is in
the coupling of the second; that the loops may take hold one
of another.

02:026:006 And thou shalt make fifty taches of gold, and couple the
curtains together with the taches: and it shall be one
tabernacle.

02:026:007 And thou shalt make curtains of goats' hair to be a covering
upon the tabernacle: eleven curtains shalt thou make.

02:026:008 The length of one curtain shall be thirty cubits, and the
breadth of one curtain four cubits: and the eleven curtains
shall be all of one measure.

02:026:009 And thou shalt couple five curtains by themselves, and six
curtains by themselves, and shalt double the sixth curtain in
the forefront of the tabernacle.

02:026:010 And thou shalt make fifty loops on the edge of the one curtain
that is outmost in the coupling, and fifty loops in the edge
of the curtain which coupleth the second.

02:026:011 And thou shalt make fifty taches of brass, and put the taches
into the loops, and couple the tent together, that it may be
one.

02:026:012 And the remnant that remaineth of the curtains of the tent, the half curtain that remaineth, shall hang over the backside of the tabernacle.

02:026:013 And a cubit on the one side, and a cubit on the other side of that which remaineth in the length of the curtains of the tent, it shall hang over the sides of the tabernacle on this side and on that side, to cover it.

02:026:014 And thou shalt make a covering for the tent of rams' skins dyed red, and a covering above of badgers' skins.

02:026:015 And thou shalt make boards for the tabernacle of shittim wood standing up.

02:026:016 Ten cubits shall be the length of a board, and a cubit and a half shall be the breadth of one board.

02:026:017 Two tenons shall there be in one board, set in order one against another: thus shalt thou make for all the boards of the tabernacle.

02:026:018 And thou shalt make the boards for the tabernacle, twenty boards on the south side southward.

02:026:019 And thou shalt make forty sockets of silver under the twenty boards; two sockets under one board for his two tenons, and two sockets under another board for his two tenons.

02:026:020 And for the second side of the tabernacle on the north side there shall be twenty boards:

02:026:021 And their forty sockets of silver; two sockets under one board, and two sockets under another board.

02:026:022 And for the sides of the tabernacle westward thou shalt make six boards.

02:026:023 And two boards shalt thou make for the corners of the tabernacle in the two sides.

02:026:024 And they shall be coupled together beneath, and they shall be
coupled together above the head of it unto one ring: thus
shall it be for them both; they shall be for the two corners.

02:026:025 And they shall be eight boards, and their sockets of silver,
sixteen sockets; two sockets under one board, and two sockets
under another board.

02:026:026 And thou shalt make bars of shittim wood; five for the boards
of the one side of the tabernacle,

02:026:027 And five bars for the boards of the other side of the
tabernacle, and five bars for the boards of the side of the
tabernacle, for the two sides westward.

02:026:028 And the middle bar in the midst of the boards shall reach from
end to end.

02:026:029 And thou shalt overlay the boards with gold, and make their
rings of gold for places for the bars: and thou shalt overlay
the bars with gold.

02:026:030 And thou shalt rear up the tabernacle according to the fashion
thereof which was shewed thee in the mount.

02:026:031 And thou shalt make a vail of blue, and purple, and scarlet,
and fine twined linen of cunning work: with cherubims shall it
be made:

02:026:032 And thou shalt hang it upon four pillars of shittim wood
overlaid with gold: their hooks shall be of gold, upon the
four sockets of silver.

02:026:033 And thou shalt hang up the vail under the taches, that thou
mayest bring in thither within the vail the ark of the
testimony: and the vail shall divide unto you between the holy
place and the most holy.

02:026:034 And thou shalt put the mercy seat upon the ark of the testimony in the most holy place.

02:026:035 And thou shalt set the table without the vail, and the candlestick over against the table on the side of the tabernacle toward the south: and thou shalt put the table on the north side.

02:026:036 And thou shalt make an hanging for the door of the tent, of blue, and purple, and scarlet, and fine twined linen, wrought with needlework.

02:026:037 And thou shalt make for the hanging five pillars of shittim wood, and overlay them with gold, and their hooks shall be of gold: and thou shalt cast five sockets of brass for them.

02:027:001 And thou shalt make an altar of shittim wood, five cubits long, and five cubits broad; the altar shall be foursquare: and the height thereof shall be three cubits.

02:027:002 And thou shalt make the horns of it upon the four corners thereof: his horns shall be of the same: and thou shalt overlay it with brass.

02:027:003 And thou shalt make his pans to receive his ashes, and his shovels, and his basons, and his fleshhooks, and his firepans: all the vessels thereof thou shalt make of brass.

02:027:004 And thou shalt make for it a grate of network of brass; and upon the net shalt thou make four brasen rings in the four corners thereof.

02:027:005 And thou shalt put it under the compass of the altar beneath, that the net may be even to the midst of the altar.

02:027:006 And thou shalt make staves for the altar, staves of shittim wood, and overlay them with brass.

02:027:007 And the staves shall be put into the rings, and the staves shall be upon the two sides of the altar, to bear it.

02:027:008 Hollow with boards shalt thou make it: as it was shewed thee in the mount, so shall they make it.

02:027:009 And thou shalt make the court of the tabernacle: for the south side southward there shall be hangings for the court of fine twined linen of an hundred cubits long for one side:

02:027:010 And the twenty pillars thereof and their twenty sockets shall be of brass; the hooks of the pillars and their fillets shall be of silver.

02:027:011 And likewise for the north side in length there shall be hangings of an hundred cubits long, and his twenty pillars and their twenty sockets of brass; the hooks of the pillars and their fillets of silver.

02:027:012 And for the breadth of the court on the west side shall be hangings of fifty cubits: their pillars ten, and their sockets ten.

02:027:013 And the breadth of the court on the east side eastward shall be fifty cubits.

02:027:014 The hangings of one side of the gate shall be fifteen cubits: their pillars three, and their sockets three.

02:027:015 And on the other side shall be hangings fifteen cubits: their pillars three, and their sockets three.

02:027:016 And for the gate of the court shall be an hanging of twenty cubits, of blue, and purple, and scarlet, and fine twined linen, wrought with needlework: and their pillars shall be four, and their sockets four.

02:027:017 All the pillars round about the court shall be filleted with silver; their hooks shall be of silver, and their sockets of brass.

02:027:018 The length of the court shall be an hundred cubits, and the
breadth fifty every where, and the height five cubits of fine
twined linen, and their sockets of brass.

02:027:019 All the vessels of the tabernacle in all the service thereof,
and all the pins thereof, and all the pins of the court, shall
be of brass.

02:027:020 And thou shalt command the children of Israel, that they bring
thee pure oil olive beaten for the light, to cause the lamp to
burn always.

02:027:021 In the tabernacle of the congregation without the vail, which
is before the testimony, Aaron and his sons shall order it
from evening to morning before the LORD: it shall be a statute
for ever unto their generations on the behalf of the children
of Israel.

02:028:001 And take thou unto thee Aaron thy brother, and his sons with
him, from among the children of Israel, that he may minister
unto me in the priest's office, even Aaron, Nadab and Abihu,
Eleazar and Ithamar, Aaron's sons.

02:028:002 And thou shalt make holy garments for Aaron thy brother for
glory and for beauty.

02:028:003 And thou shalt speak unto all that are wise hearted, whom I
have filled with the spirit of wisdom, that they may make
Aaron's garments to consecrate him, that he may minister unto
me in the priest's office.

02:028:004 And these are the garments which they shall make; a
breastplate, and an ephod, and a robe, and a broidered coat, a
mitre, and a girdle: and they shall make holy garments for
Aaron thy brother, and his sons, that he may minister unto me
in the priest's office.

02:028:005 And they shall take gold, and blue, and purple, and scarlet, and fine linen.

02:028:006 And they shall make the ephod of gold, of blue, and of purple, of scarlet, and fine twined linen, with cunning work.

02:028:007 It shall have the two shoulderpieces thereof joined at the two edges thereof; and so it shall be joined together.

02:028:008 And the curious girdle of the ephod, which is upon it, shall be of the same, according to the work thereof; even of gold, of blue, and purple, and scarlet, and fine twined linen.

02:028:009 And thou shalt take two onyx stones, and grave on them the names of the children of Israel:

02:028:010 Six of their names on one stone, and the other six names of the rest on the other stone, according to their birth.

02:028:011 With the work of an engraver in stone, like the engravings of a signet, shalt thou engrave the two stones with the names of the children of Israel: thou shalt make them to be set in ouches of gold.

02:028:012 And thou shalt put the two stones upon the shoulders of the ephod for stones of memorial unto the children of Israel: and Aaron shall bear their names before the LORD upon his two shoulders for a memorial.

02:028:013 And thou shalt make ouches of gold;

02:028:014 And two chains of pure gold at the ends; of wreathen work shalt thou make them, and fasten the wreathen chains to the ouches.

02:028:015 And thou shalt make the breastplate of judgment with cunning work; after the work of the ephod thou shalt make it; of gold, of blue, and of purple, and of scarlet, and of fine twined linen, shalt thou make it.

02:028:016 Foursquare it shall be being doubled; a span shall be the length thereof, and a span shall be the breadth thereof.

02:028:017 And thou shalt set in it settings of stones, even four rows of stones: the first row shall be a sardius, a topaz, and a carbuncle: this shall be the first row.

02:028:018 And the second row shall be an emerald, a sapphire, and a diamond.

02:028:019 And the third row a ligure, an agate, and an amethyst.

02:028:020 And the fourth row a beryl, and an onyx, and a jasper: they shall be set in gold in their inclosings.

02:028:021 And the stones shall be with the names of the children of Israel, twelve, according to their names, like the engravings of a signet; every one with his name shall they be according to the twelve tribes.

02:028:022 And thou shalt make upon the breastplate chains at the ends of wreathen work of pure gold.

02:028:023 And thou shalt make upon the breastplate two rings of gold, and shalt put the two rings on the two ends of the breastplate.

02:028:024 And thou shalt put the two wreathen chains of gold in the two rings which are on the ends of the breastplate.

02:028:025 And the other two ends of the two wreathen chains thou shalt fasten in the two ouches, and put them on the shoulderpieces of the ephod before it.

02:028:026 And thou shalt make two rings of gold, and thou shalt put them upon the two ends of the breastplate in the border thereof, which is in the side of the ephod inward.

02:028:027 And two other rings of gold thou shalt make, and shalt put

them on the two sides of the ephod underneath, toward the
forepart thereof, over against the other coupling thereof,
above the curious girdle of the ephod.

02:028:028 And they shall bind the breastplate by the rings thereof unto
the rings of the ephod with a lace of blue, that it may be
above the curious girdle of the ephod, and that the
breastplate be not loosed from the ephod.

02:028:029 And Aaron shall bear the names of the children of Israel in
the breastplate of judgment upon his heart, when he goeth in
unto the holy place, for a memorial before the LORD
continually.

02:028:030 And thou shalt put in the breastplate of judgment the Urim and
the Thummim; and they shall be upon Aaron's heart, when he
goeth in before the LORD: and Aaron shall bear the judgment of
the children of Israel upon his heart before the LORD
continually.

02:028:031 And thou shalt make the robe of the ephod all of blue.

02:028:032 And there shall be an hole in the top of it, in the midst
thereof: it shall have a binding of woven work round about the
hole of it, as it were the hole of an habergeon, that it be
not rent.

02:028:033 And beneath upon the hem of it thou shalt make pomegranates of
blue, and of purple, and of scarlet, round about the hem
thereof; and bells of gold between them round about:

02:028:034 A golden bell and a pomegranate, a golden bell and a
pomegranate, upon the hem of the robe round about.

02:028:035 And it shall be upon Aaron to minister: and his sound shall be
heard when he goeth in unto the holy place before the LORD,
and when he cometh out, that he die not.

02:028:036 And thou shalt make a plate of pure gold, and grave upon it, like the engravings of a signet, HOLINESS TO THE LORD.

02:028:037 And thou shalt put it on a blue lace, that it may be upon the mitre; upon the forefront of the mitre it shall be.

02:028:038 And it shall be upon Aaron's forehead, that Aaron may bear the iniquity of the holy things, which the children of Israel shall hallow in all their holy gifts; and it shall be always upon his forehead, that they may be accepted before the LORD.

02:028:039 And thou shalt embroider the coat of fine linen, and thou shalt make the mitre of fine linen, and thou shalt make the girdle of needlework.

02:028:040 And for Aaron's sons thou shalt make coats, and thou shalt make for them girdles, and bonnets shalt thou make for them, for glory and for beauty.

02:028:041 And thou shalt put them upon Aaron thy brother, and his sons with him; and shalt anoint them, and consecrate them, and sanctify them, that they may minister unto me in the priest's office.

02:028:042 And thou shalt make them linen breeches to cover their nakedness; from the loins even unto the thighs they shall reach:

02:028:043 And they shall be upon Aaron, and upon his sons, when they come in unto the tabernacle of the congregation, or when they come near unto the altar to minister in the holy place; that they bear not iniquity, and die: it shall be a statute for ever unto him and his seed after him.

02:029:001 And this is the thing that thou shalt do unto them to hallow them, to minister unto me in the priest's office: Take one young bullock, and two rams without blemish,

02:029:002 And unleavened bread, and cakes unleavened tempered with oil, and wafers unleavened anointed with oil: of wheaten flour shalt thou make them.

02:029:003 And thou shalt put them into one basket, and bring them in the basket, with the bullock and the two rams.

02:029:004 And Aaron and his sons thou shalt bring unto the door of the tabernacle of the congregation, and shalt wash them with water.

02:029:005 And thou shalt take the garments, and put upon Aaron the coat, and the robe of the ephod, and the ephod, and the breastplate, and gird him with the curious girdle of the ephod:

02:029:006 And thou shalt put the mitre upon his head, and put the holy crown upon the mitre.

02:029:007 Then shalt thou take the anointing oil, and pour it upon his head, and anoint him.

02:029:008 And thou shalt bring his sons, and put coats upon them.

02:029:009 And thou shalt gird them with girdles, Aaron and his sons, and put the bonnets on them: and the priest's office shall be theirs for a perpetual statute: and thou shalt consecrate Aaron and his sons.

02:029:010 And thou shalt cause a bullock to be brought before the tabernacle of the congregation: and Aaron and his sons shall put their hands upon the head of the bullock.

02:029:011 And thou shalt kill the bullock before the LORD, by the door of the tabernacle of the congregation.

02:029:012 And thou shalt take of the blood of the bullock, and put it upon the horns of the altar with thy finger, and pour all the blood beside the bottom of the altar.

02:029:013 And thou shalt take all the fat that covereth the inwards, and the caul that is above the liver, and the two kidneys, and the fat that is upon them, and burn them upon the altar.

02:029:014 But the flesh of the bullock, and his skin, and his dung, shalt thou burn with fire without the camp: it is a sin offering.

02:029:015 Thou shalt also take one ram; and Aaron and his sons shall put their hands upon the head of the ram.

02:029:016 And thou shalt slay the ram, and thou shalt take his blood, and sprinkle it round about upon the altar.

02:029:017 And thou shalt cut the ram in pieces, and wash the inwards of him, and his legs, and put them unto his pieces, and unto his head.

02:029:018 And thou shalt burn the whole ram upon the altar: it is a burnt offering unto the LORD: it is a sweet savour, an offering made by fire unto the LORD.

02:029:019 And thou shalt take the other ram; and Aaron and his sons shall put their hands upon the head of the ram.

02:029:020 Then shalt thou kill the ram, and take of his blood, and put it upon the tip of the right ear of Aaron, and upon the tip of the right ear of his sons, and upon the thumb of their right hand, and upon the great toe of their right foot, and sprinkle the blood upon the altar round about.

02:029:021 And thou shalt take of the blood that is upon the altar, and of the anointing oil, and sprinkle it upon Aaron, and upon his garments, and upon his sons, and upon the garments of his sons with him: and he shall be hallowed, and his garments, and his sons, and his sons' garments with him.

02:029:022 Also thou shalt take of the ram the fat and the rump, and the fat that covereth the inwards, and the caul above the liver, and the two kidneys, and the fat that is upon them, and the right shoulder; for it is a ram of consecration:

02:029:023 And one loaf of bread, and one cake of oiled bread, and one wafer out of the basket of the unleavened bread that is before the LORD:

02:029:024 And thou shalt put all in the hands of Aaron, and in the hands of his sons; and shalt wave them for a wave offering before the LORD.

02:029:025 And thou shalt receive them of their hands, and burn them upon the altar for a burnt offering, for a sweet savour before the LORD: it is an offering made by fire unto the LORD.

02:029:026 And thou shalt take the breast of the ram of Aaron's consecration, and wave it for a wave offering before the LORD: and it shall be thy part.

02:029:027 And thou shalt sanctify the breast of the wave offering, and the shoulder of the heave offering, which is waved, and which is heaved up, of the ram of the consecration, even of that which is for Aaron, and of that which is for his sons:

02:029:028 And it shall be Aaron's and his sons' by a statute for ever from the children of Israel: for it is an heave offering: and it shall be an heave offering from the children of Israel of the sacrifice of their peace offerings, even their heave offering unto the LORD.

02:029:029 And the holy garments of Aaron shall be his sons' after him, to be anointed therein, and to be consecrated in them.

02:029:030 And that son that is priest in his stead shall put them on seven days, when he cometh into the tabernacle of the congregation to minister in the holy place.

02:029:031 And thou shalt take the ram of the consecration, and seethe his flesh in the holy place.

02:029:032 And Aaron and his sons shall eat the flesh of the ram, and the bread that is in the basket by the door of the tabernacle of the congregation.

02:029:033 And they shall eat those things wherewith the atonement was
made, to consecrate and to sanctify them: but a stranger shall
not eat thereof, because they are holy.

02:029:034 And if ought of the flesh of the consecrations, or of the
bread, remain unto the morning, then thou shalt burn the
remainder with fire: it shall not be eaten, because it is
holy.

02:029:035 And thus shalt thou do unto Aaron, and to his sons, according
to all things which I have commanded thee: seven days shalt
thou consecrate them.

02:029:036 And thou shalt offer every day a bullock for a sin offering
for atonement: and thou shalt cleanse the altar, when thou
hast made an atonement for it, and thou shalt anoint it, to
sanctify it.

02:029:037 Seven days thou shalt make an atonement for the altar, and
sanctify it; and it shall be an altar most holy: whatsoever
toucheth the altar shall be holy.

02:029:038 Now this is that which thou shalt offer upon the altar; two
lambs of the first year day by day continually.

02:029:039 The one lamb thou shalt offer in the morning; and the other
lamb thou shalt offer at even:

02:029:040 And with the one lamb a tenth deal of flour mingled with the
fourth part of an hin of beaten oil; and the fourth part of an
hin of wine for a drink offering.

02:029:041 And the other lamb thou shalt offer at even, and shalt do
thereto according to the meat offering of the morning, and
according to the drink offering thereof, for a sweet savour,
an offering made by fire unto the LORD.

02:029:042 This shall be a continual burnt offering throughout your generations at the door of the tabernacle of the congregation before the LORD: where I will meet you, to speak there unto thee.

02:029:043 And there I will meet with the children of Israel, and the tabernacle shall be sanctified by my glory.

02:029:044 And I will sanctify the tabernacle of the congregation, and the altar: I will sanctify also both Aaron and his sons, to minister to me in the priest's office.

02:029:045 And I will dwell among the children of Israel, and will be their God.

02:029:046 And they shall know that I am the LORD their God, that brought them forth out of the land of Egypt, that I may dwell among them: I am the LORD their God.

02:030:001 And thou shalt make an altar to burn incense upon: of shittim wood shalt thou make it.

02:030:002 A cubit shall be the length thereof, and a cubit the breadth thereof; foursquare shall it be: and two cubits shall be the height thereof: the horns thereof shall be of the same.

02:030:003 And thou shalt overlay it with pure gold, the top thereof, and the sides thereof round about, and the horns thereof; and thou shalt make unto it a crown of gold round about.

02:030:004 And two golden rings shalt thou make to it under the crown of it, by the two corners thereof, upon the two sides of it shalt thou make it; and they shall be for places for the staves to bear it withal.

02:030:005 And thou shalt make the staves of shittim wood, and overlay them with gold.

02:030:006 And thou shalt put it before the vail that is by the ark of

the testimony, before the mercy seat that is over the
testimony, where I will meet with thee.

02:030:007 And Aaron shall burn thereon sweet incense every morning: when
he dresseth the lamps, he shall burn incense upon it.

02:030:008 And when Aaron lighteth the lamps at even, he shall burn
incense upon it, a perpetual incense before the LORD
throughout your generations.

02:030:009 Ye shall offer no strange incense thereon, nor burnt
sacrifice, nor meat offering; neither shall ye pour drink
offering thereon.

02:030:010 And Aaron shall make an atonement upon the horns of it once in
a year with the blood of the sin offering of atonements: once
in the year shall he make atonement upon it throughout your
generations: it is most holy unto the LORD.

02:030:011 And the LORD spake unto Moses, saying,

02:030:012 When thou takest the sum of the children of Israel after their
number, then shall they give every man a ransom for his soul
unto the LORD, when thou numberest them; that there be no
plague among them, when thou numberest them.

02:030:013 This they shall give, every one that passeth among them that
are numbered, half a shekel after the shekel of the sanctuary:
(a shekel is twenty gerahs:) an half shekel shall be the
offering of the LORD.

02:030:014 Every one that passeth among them that are numbered, from
twenty years old and above, shall give an offering unto the
LORD.

02:030:015 The rich shall not give more, and the poor shall not give less
than half a shekel, when they give an offering unto the LORD,
to make an atonement for your souls.

02:030:016 And thou shalt take the atonement money of the children of
Israel, and shalt appoint it for the service of the tabernacle
of the congregation; that it may be a memorial unto the
children of Israel before the LORD, to make an atonement for
your souls.

02:030:017 And the LORD spake unto Moses, saying,

02:030:018 Thou shalt also make a laver of brass, and his foot also of
brass, to wash withal: and thou shalt put it between the
tabernacle of the congregation and the altar, and thou shalt
put water therein.

02:030:019 For Aaron and his sons shall wash their hands and their feet
thereat:

02:030:020 When they go into the tabernacle of the congregation, they
shall wash with water, that they die not; or when they come
near to the altar to minister, to burn offering made by fire
unto the LORD:

02:030:021 So they shall wash their hands and their feet, that they die
not: and it shall be a statute for ever to them, even to him
and to his seed throughout their generations.

02:030:022 Moreover the LORD spake unto Moses, saying,

02:030:023 Take thou also unto thee principal spices, of pure myrrh five
hundred shekels, and of sweet cinnamon half so much, even two
hundred and fifty shekels, and of sweet calamus two hundred
and fifty shekels,

02:030:024 And of cassia five hundred shekels, after the shekel of the
sanctuary, and of oil olive an hin:

02:030:025 And thou shalt make it an oil of holy ointment, an ointment
compound after the art of the apothecary: it shall be an holy
anointing oil.

02:030:026 And thou shalt anoint the tabernacle of the congregation therewith, and the ark of the testimony,

02:030:027 And the table and all his vessels, and the candlestick and his vessels, and the altar of incense,

02:030:028 And the altar of burnt offering with all his vessels, and the laver and his foot.

02:030:029 And thou shalt sanctify them, that they may be most holy: whatsoever toucheth them shall be holy.

02:030:030 And thou shalt anoint Aaron and his sons, and consecrate them, that they may minister unto me in the priest's office.

02:030:031 And thou shalt speak unto the children of Israel, saying, This shall be an holy anointing oil unto me throughout your generations.

02:030:032 Upon man's flesh shall it not be poured, neither shall ye make any other like it, after the composition of it: it is holy, and it shall be holy unto you.

02:030:033 Whosoever compoundeth any like it, or whosoever putteth any of it upon a stranger, shall even be cut off from his people.

02:030:034 And the LORD said unto Moses, Take unto thee sweet spices, stacte, and onycha, and galbanum; these sweet spices with pure frankincense: of each shall there be a like weight:

02:030:035 And thou shalt make it a perfume, a confection after the art of the apothecary, tempered together, pure and holy:

02:030:036 And thou shalt beat some of it very small, and put of it before the testimony in the tabernacle of the congregation, where I will meet with thee: it shall be unto you most holy.

02:030:037 And as for the perfume which thou shalt make, ye shall not make to yourselves according to the composition thereof: it shall be unto thee holy for the LORD.

02:030:038 Whosoever shall make like unto that, to smell thereto, shall even be cut off from his people.

02:031:001 And the LORD spake unto Moses, saying,

02:031:002 See, I have called by name Bezaleel the son of Uri, the son of Hur, of the tribe of Judah:

02:031:003 And I have filled him with the spirit of God, in wisdom, and in understanding, and in knowledge, and in all manner of workmanship,

02:031:004 To devise cunning works, to work in gold, and in silver, and in brass,

02:031:005 And in cutting of stones, to set them, and in carving of timber, to work in all manner of workmanship.

02:031:006 And I, behold, I have given with him Aholiab, the son of Ahisamach, of the tribe of Dan: and in the hearts of all that are wise hearted I have put wisdom, that they may make all that I have commanded thee;

02:031:007 The tabernacle of the congregation, and the ark of the testimony, and the mercy seat that is thereupon, and all the furniture of the tabernacle,

02:031:008 And the table and his furniture, and the pure candlestick with all his furniture, and the altar of incense,

02:031:009 And the altar of burnt offering with all his furniture, and the laver and his foot,

02:031:010 And the cloths of service, and the holy garments for Aaron the priest, and the garments of his sons, to minister in the priest's office,

02:031:011 And the anointing oil, and sweet incense for the holy place: according to all that I have commanded thee shall they do.

02:031:012 And the LORD spake unto Moses, saying,

02:031:013 Speak thou also unto the children of Israel, saying, Verily my sabbaths ye shall keep: for it is a sign between me and you throughout your generations; that ye may know that I am the LORD that doth sanctify you.

02:031:014 Ye shall keep the sabbath therefore; for it is holy unto you: every one that defileth it shall surely be put to death: for whosoever doeth any work therein, that soul shall be cut off from among his people.

02:031:015 Six days may work be done; but in the seventh is the sabbath of rest, holy to the LORD: whosoever doeth any work in the sabbath day, he shall surely be put to death.

02:031:016 Wherefore the children of Israel shall keep the sabbath, to observe the sabbath throughout their generations, for a perpetual covenant.

02:031:017 It is a sign between me and the children of Israel for ever: for in six days the LORD made heaven and earth, and on the seventh day he rested, and was refreshed.

02:031:018 And he gave unto Moses, when he had made an end of communing with him upon mount Sinai, two tables of testimony, tables of stone, written with the finger of God.

02:032:001 And when the people saw that Moses delayed to come down out of the mount, the people gathered themselves together unto Aaron, and said unto him, Up, make us gods, which shall go before us; for as for this Moses, the man that brought us up out of the land of Egypt, we wot not what is become of him.

02:032:002 And Aaron said unto them, Break off the golden earrings, which are in the ears of your wives, of your sons, and of your daughters, and bring them unto me.

02:032:003 And all the people brake off the golden earrings which were in their ears, and brought them unto Aaron.

02:032:004 And he received them at their hand, and fashioned it with a graving tool, after he had made it a molten calf: and they said, These be thy gods, O Israel, which brought thee up out of the land of Egypt.

02:032:005 And when Aaron saw it, he built an altar before it; and Aaron made proclamation, and said, To morrow is a feast to the LORD.

02:032:006 And they rose up early on the morrow, and offered burnt offerings, and brought peace offerings; and the people sat down to eat and to drink, and rose up to play.

02:032:007 And the LORD said unto Moses, Go, get thee down; for thy people, which thou broughtest out of the land of Egypt, have corrupted themselves:

02:032:008 They have turned aside quickly out of the way which I commanded them: they have made them a molten calf, and have worshipped it, and have sacrificed thereunto, and said, These be thy gods, O Israel, which have brought thee up out of the land of Egypt.

02:032:009 And the LORD said unto Moses, I have seen this people, and, behold, it is a stiffnecked people:

02:032:010 Now therefore let me alone, that my wrath may wax hot against them, and that I may consume them: and I will make of thee a great nation.

02:032:011 And Moses besought the LORD his God, and said, LORD, why doth thy wrath wax hot against thy people, which thou hast brought forth out of the land of Egypt with great power, and with a mighty hand?

02:032:012 Wherefore should the Egyptians speak, and say, For mischief
did he bring them out, to slay them in the mountains, and to
consume them from the face of the earth? Turn from thy fierce
wrath, and repent of this evil against thy people.

02:032:013 Remember Abraham, Isaac, and Israel, thy servants, to whom
thou swarest by thine own self, and saidst unto them, I will
multiply your seed as the stars of heaven, and all this land
that I have spoken of will I give unto your seed, and they
shall inherit it for ever.

02:032:014 And the LORD repented of the evil which he thought to do unto
his people.

02:032:015 And Moses turned, and went down from the mount, and the two
tables of the testimony were in his hand: the tables were
written on both their sides; on the one side and on the other
were they written.

02:032:016 And the tables were the work of God, and the writing was the
writing of God, graven upon the tables.

02:032:017 And when Joshua heard the noise of the people as they shouted,
he said unto Moses, There is a noise of war in the camp.

02:032:018 And he said, It is not the voice of them that shout for
mastery, neither is it the voice of them that cry for being
overcome: but the noise of them that sing do I hear.

02:032:019 And it came to pass, as soon as he came nigh unto the camp,
that he saw the calf, and the dancing: and Moses' anger waxed
hot, and he cast the tables out of his hands, and brake them
beneath the mount.

02:032:020 And he took the calf which they had made, and burnt it in the
fire, and ground it to powder, and strawed it upon the water,
and made the children of Israel drink of it.

02:032:021 And Moses said unto Aaron, What did this people unto thee, that thou hast brought so great a sin upon them?

02:032:022 And Aaron said, Let not the anger of my lord wax hot: thou knowest the people, that they are set on mischief.

02:032:023 For they said unto me, Make us gods, which shall go before us: for as for this Moses, the man that brought us up out of the land of Egypt, we wot not what is become of him.

02:032:024 And I said unto them, Whosoever hath any gold, let them break it off. So they gave it me: then I cast it into the fire, and there came out this calf.

02:032:025 And when Moses saw that the people were naked; (for Aaron had made them naked unto their shame among their enemies:)

02:032:026 Then Moses stood in the gate of the camp, and said, Who is on the LORD's side? let him come unto me. And all the sons of Levi gathered themselves together unto him.

02:032:027 And he said unto them, Thus saith the LORD God of Israel, Put every man his sword by his side, and go in and out from gate to gate throughout the camp, and slay every man his brother, and every man his companion, and every man his neighbour.

02:032:028 And the children of Levi did according to the word of Moses: and there fell of the people that day about three thousand men.

02:032:029 For Moses had said, Consecrate yourselves today to the LORD, even every man upon his son, and upon his brother; that he may bestow upon you a blessing this day.

02:032:030 And it came to pass on the morrow, that Moses said unto the people, Ye have sinned a great sin: and now I will go up unto the LORD; peradventure I shall make an atonement for your sin.

02:032:031 And Moses returned unto the LORD, and said, Oh, this people have sinned a great sin, and have made them gods of gold.

02:032:032 Yet now, if thou wilt forgive their sin--; and if not, blot
me, I pray thee, out of thy book which thou hast written.

02:032:033 And the LORD said unto Moses, Whosoever hath sinned against
me, him will I blot out of my book.

02:032:034 Therefore now go, lead the people unto the place of which I
have spoken unto thee: behold, mine Angel shall go before
thee: nevertheless in the day when I visit I will visit their
sin upon them.

02:032:035 And the LORD plagued the people, because they made the calf,
which Aaron made.

02:033:001 And the LORD said unto Moses, Depart, and go up hence, thou
and the people which thou hast brought up out of the land of
Egypt, unto the land which I sware unto Abraham, to Isaac, and
to Jacob, saying, Unto thy seed will I give it:

02:033:002 And I will send an angel before thee; and I will drive out the
Canaanite, the Amorite, and the Hittite, and the Perizzite,
the Hivite, and the Jebusite:

02:033:003 Unto a land flowing with milk and honey: for I will not go up
in the midst of thee; for thou art a stiffnecked people: lest
I consume thee in the way.

02:033:004 And when the people heard these evil tidings, they mourned:
and no man did put on him his ornaments.

02:033:005 For the LORD had said unto Moses, Say unto the children of
Israel, Ye are a stiffnecked people: I will come up into the
midst of thee in a moment, and consume thee: therefore now put
off thy ornaments from thee, that I may know what to do unto
thee.

02:033:006 And the children of Israel stripped themselves of their
ornaments by the mount Horeb.

02:033:007 And Moses took the tabernacle, and pitched it without the camp, afar off from the camp, and called it the Tabernacle of the congregation. And it came to pass, that every one which sought the LORD went out unto the tabernacle of the congregation, which was without the camp.

02:033:008 And it came to pass, when Moses went out unto the tabernacle, that all the people rose up, and stood every man at his tent door, and looked after Moses, until he was gone into the tabernacle.

02:033:009 And it came to pass, as Moses entered into the tabernacle, the cloudy pillar descended, and stood at the door of the tabernacle, and the Lord talked with Moses.

02:033:010 And all the people saw the cloudy pillar stand at the tabernacle door: and all the people rose up and worshipped, every man in his tent door.

02:033:011 And the LORD spake unto Moses face to face, as a man speaketh unto his friend. And he turned again into the camp: but his servant Joshua, the son of Nun, a young man, departed not out of the tabernacle.

02:033:012 And Moses said unto the LORD, See, thou sayest unto me, Bring up this people: and thou hast not let me know whom thou wilt send with me. Yet thou hast said, I know thee by name, and thou hast also found grace in my sight.

02:033:013 Now therefore, I pray thee, if I have found grace in thy sight, shew me now thy way, that I may know thee, that I may find grace in thy sight: and consider that this nation is thy people.

02:033:014 And he said, My presence shall go with thee, and I will give thee rest.

02:033:015 And he said unto him, If thy presence go not with me, carry us not up hence.

02:033:016 For wherein shall it be known here that I and thy people have
found grace in thy sight? is it not in that thou goest with
us? so shall we be separated, I and thy people, from all the
people that are upon the face of the earth.

02:033:017 And the LORD said unto Moses, I will do this thing also that
thou hast spoken: for thou hast found grace in my sight, and I
know thee by name.

02:033:018 And he said, I beseech thee, shew me thy glory.

02:033:019 And he said, I will make all my goodness pass before thee, and
I will proclaim the name of the LORD before thee; and will be
gracious to whom I will be gracious, and will shew mercy on
whom I will shew mercy.

02:033:020 And he said, Thou canst not see my face: for there shall no
man see me, and live.

02:033:021 And the LORD said, Behold, there is a place by me, and thou
shalt stand upon a rock:

02:033:022 And it shall come to pass, while my glory passeth by, that I
will put thee in a clift of the rock, and will cover thee with
my hand while I pass by:

02:033:023 And I will take away mine hand, and thou shalt see my back
parts: but my face shall not be seen.

02:034:001 And the LORD said unto Moses, Hew thee two tables of stone
like unto the first: and I will write upon these tables the
words that were in the first tables, which thou brakest.

02:034:002 And be ready in the morning, and come up in the morning unto
mount Sinai, and present thyself there to me in the top of the
mount.

02:034:003 And no man shall come up with thee, neither let any man be
seen throughout all the mount; neither let the flocks nor
herds feed before that mount.

02:034:004 And he hewed two tables of stone like unto the first; and
Moses rose up early in the morning, and went up unto mount
Sinai, as the LORD had commanded him, and took in his hand the
two tables of stone.

02:034:005 And the LORD descended in the cloud, and stood with him there,
and proclaimed the name of the LORD.

02:034:006 And the LORD passed by before him, and proclaimed, The LORD,
The LORD God, merciful and gracious, longsuffering, and
abundant in goodness and truth,

02:034:007 Keeping mercy for thousands, forgiving iniquity and
transgression and sin, and that will by no means clear the
guilty; visiting the iniquity of the fathers upon the
children, and upon the children's children, unto the third and
to the fourth generation.

02:034:008 And Moses made haste, and bowed his head toward the earth, and
worshipped.

02:034:009 And he said, If now I have found grace in thy sight, O LORD,
let my LORD, I pray thee, go among us; for it is a stiffnecked
people; and pardon our iniquity and our sin, and take us for
thine inheritance.

02:034:010 And he said, Behold, I make a covenant: before all thy people
I will do marvels, such as have not been done in all the
earth, nor in any nation: and all the people among which thou
art shall see the work of the LORD: for it is a terrible thing
that I will do with thee.

02:034:011 Observe thou that which I command thee this day: behold, I
drive out before thee the Amorite, and the Canaanite, and the

Hittite, and the Perizzite, and the Hivite, and the Jebusite.

02:034:012 Take heed to thyself, lest thou make a covenant with the
inhabitants of the land whither thou goest, lest it be for a
snare in the midst of thee:

02:034:013 But ye shall destroy their altars, break their images, and cut
down their groves:

02:034:014 For thou shalt worship no other god: for the LORD, whose name
is Jealous, is a jealous God:

02:034:015 Lest thou make a covenant with the inhabitants of the land,
and they go a whoring after their gods, and do sacrifice unto
their gods, and one call thee, and thou eat of his sacrifice;

02:034:016 And thou take of their daughters unto thy sons, and their
daughters go a whoring after their gods, and make thy sons go
a whoring after their gods.

02:034:017 Thou shalt make thee no molten gods.

02:034:018 The feast of unleavened bread shalt thou keep. Seven days thou
shalt eat unleavened bread, as I commanded thee, in the time
of the month Abib: for in the month Abib thou camest out from
Egypt.

02:034:019 All that openeth the matrix is mine; and every firstling among
thy cattle, whether ox or sheep, that is male.

02:034:020 But the firstling of an ass thou shalt redeem with a lamb: and
if thou redeem him not, then shalt thou break his neck. All
the firstborn of thy sons thou shalt redeem. And none shall
appear before me empty.

02:034:021 Six days thou shalt work, but on the seventh day thou shalt
rest: in earing time and in harvest thou shalt rest.

02:034:022 And thou shalt observe the feast of weeks, of the firstfruits

of wheat harvest, and the feast of ingathering at the year's
end.

02:034:023 Thrice in the year shall all your menchildren appear before
the LORD God, the God of Israel.

02:034:024 For I will cast out the nations before thee, and enlarge thy
borders: neither shall any man desire thy land, when thou
shalt go up to appear before the LORD thy God thrice in the
year.

02:034:025 Thou shalt not offer the blood of my sacrifice with leaven;
neither shall the sacrifice of the feast of the passover be
left unto the morning.

02:034:026 The first of the firstfruits of thy land thou shalt bring unto
the house of the LORD thy God. Thou shalt not seethe a kid in
his mother's milk.

02:034:027 And the LORD said unto Moses, Write thou these words: for
after the tenor of these words I have made a covenant with
thee and with Israel.

02:034:028 And he was there with the LORD forty days and forty nights; he
did neither eat bread, nor drink water. And he wrote upon the
tables the words of the covenant, the ten commandments.

02:034:029 And it came to pass, when Moses came down from mount Sinai
with the two tables of testimony in Moses' hand, when he came
down from the mount, that Moses wist not that the skin of his
face shone while he talked with him.

02:034:030 And when Aaron and all the children of Israel saw Moses,
behold, the skin of his face shone; and they were afraid to
come nigh him.

02:034:031 And Moses called unto them; and Aaron and all the rulers of
the congregation returned unto him: and Moses talked with
them.

02:034:032 And afterward all the children of Israel came nigh: and he gave them in commandment all that the LORD had spoken with him in mount Sinai.

02:034:033 And till Moses had done speaking with them, he put a vail on his face.

02:034:034 But when Moses went in before the LORD to speak with him, he took the vail off, until he came out. And he came out, and spake unto the children of Israel that which he was commanded.

02:034:035 And the children of Israel saw the face of Moses, that the skin of Moses' face shone: and Moses put the vail upon his face again, until he went in to speak with him.

02:035:001 And Moses gathered all the congregation of the children of Israel together, and said unto them, These are the words which the LORD hath commanded, that ye should do them.

02:035:002 Six days shall work be done, but on the seventh day there shall be to you an holy day, a sabbath of rest to the LORD: whosoever doeth work therein shall be put to death.

02:035:003 Ye shall kindle no fire throughout your habitations upon the sabbath day.

02:035:004 And Moses spake unto all the congregation of the children of Israel, saying, This is the thing which the LORD commanded, saying,

02:035:005 Take ye from among you an offering unto the LORD: whosoever is of a willing heart, let him bring it, an offering of the LORD; gold, and silver, and brass,

02:035:006 And blue, and purple, and scarlet, and fine linen, and goats' hair,

02:035:007 And rams' skins dyed red, and badgers' skins, and shittim wood,

02:035:008 And oil for the light, and spices for anointing oil, and for the sweet incense,

02:035:009 And onyx stones, and stones to be set for the ephod, and for the breastplate.

02:035:010 And every wise hearted among you shall come, and make all that the LORD hath commanded;

02:035:011 The tabernacle, his tent, and his covering, his taches, and his boards, his bars, his pillars, and his sockets,

02:035:012 The ark, and the staves thereof, with the mercy seat, and the vail of the covering,

02:035:013 The table, and his staves, and all his vessels, and the shewbread,

02:035:014 The candlestick also for the light, and his furniture, and his lamps, with the oil for the light,

02:035:015 And the incense altar, and his staves, and the anointing oil, and the sweet incense, and the hanging for the door at the entering in of the tabernacle,

02:035:016 The altar of burnt offering, with his brasen grate, his staves, and all his vessels, the laver and his foot,

02:035:017 The hangings of the court, his pillars, and their sockets, and the hanging for the door of the court,

02:035:018 The pins of the tabernacle, and the pins of the court, and their cords,

02:035:019 The cloths of service, to do service in the holy place, the holy garments for Aaron the priest, and the garments of his sons, to minister in the priest's office.

02:035:020 And all the congregation of the children of Israel departed from the presence of Moses.

02:035:021 And they came, every one whose heart stirred him up, and every
one whom his spirit made willing, and they brought the LORD's
offering to the work of the tabernacle of the congregation,
and for all his service, and for the holy garments.

02:035:022 And they came, both men and women, as many as were willing
hearted, and brought bracelets, and earrings, and rings, and
tablets, all jewels of gold: and every man that offered
offered an offering of gold unto the LORD.

02:035:023 And every man, with whom was found blue, and purple, and
scarlet, and fine linen, and goats' hair, and red skins of
rams, and badgers' skins, brought them.

02:035:024 Every one that did offer an offering of silver and brass
brought the LORD's offering: and every man, with whom was
found shittim wood for any work of the service, brought it.

02:035:025 And all the women that were wise hearted did spin with their
hands, and brought that which they had spun, both of blue, and
of purple, and of scarlet, and of fine linen.

02:035:026 And all the women whose heart stirred them up in wisdom spun
goats' hair.

02:035:027 And the rulers brought onyx stones, and stones to be set, for
the ephod, and for the breastplate;

02:035:028 And spice, and oil for the light, and for the anointing oil,
and for the sweet incense.

02:035:029 The children of Israel brought a willing offering unto the
LORD, every man and woman, whose heart made them willing to
bring for all manner of work, which the LORD had commanded to
be made by the hand of Moses.

02:035:030 And Moses said unto the children of Israel, See, the LORD hath called by name Bezaleel the son of Uri, the son of Hur, of the tribe of Judah;

02:035:031 And he hath filled him with the spirit of God, in wisdom, in understanding, and in knowledge, and in all manner of workmanship;

02:035:032 And to devise curious works, to work in gold, and in silver, and in brass,

02:035:033 And in the cutting of stones, to set them, and in carving of wood, to make any manner of cunning work.

02:035:034 And he hath put in his heart that he may teach, both he, and Aholiab, the son of Ahisamach, of the tribe of Dan.

02:035:035 Them hath he filled with wisdom of heart, to work all manner of work, of the engraver, and of the cunning workman, and of the embroiderer, in blue, and in purple, in scarlet, and in fine linen, and of the weaver, even of them that do any work, and of those that devise cunning work.

02:036:001 Then wrought Bezaleel and Aholiab, and every wise hearted man, in whom the LORD put wisdom and understanding to know how to work all manner of work for the service of the sanctuary, according to all that the LORD had commanded.

02:036:002 And Moses called Bezaleel and Aholiab, and every wise hearted man, in whose heart the LORD had put wisdom, even every one whose heart stirred him up to come unto the work to do it:

02:036:003 And they received of Moses all the offering, which the children of Israel had brought for the work of the service of the sanctuary, to make it withal. And they brought yet unto him free offerings every morning.

02:036:004 And all the wise men, that wrought all the work of the sanctuary, came every man from his work which they made;

02:036:005 And they spake unto Moses, saying, The people bring much more
than enough for the service of the work, which the LORD
commanded to make.

02:036:006 And Moses gave commandment, and they caused it to be
proclaimed throughout the camp, saying, Let neither man nor
woman make any more work for the offering of the sanctuary. So
the people were restrained from bringing.

02:036:007 For the stuff they had was sufficient for all the work to make
it, and too much.

02:036:008 And every wise hearted man among them that wrought the work of
the tabernacle made ten curtains of fine twined linen, and
blue, and purple, and scarlet: with cherubims of cunning work
made he them.

02:036:009 The length of one curtain was twenty and eight cubits, and the
breadth of one curtain four cubits: the curtains were all of
one size.

02:036:010 And he coupled the five curtains one unto another: and the
other five curtains he coupled one unto another.

02:036:011 And he made loops of blue on the edge of one curtain from the
selvedge in the coupling: likewise he made in the uttermost
side of another curtain, in the coupling of the second.

02:036:012 Fifty loops made he in one curtain, and fifty loops made he in
the edge of the curtain which was in the coupling of the
second: the loops held one curtain to another.

02:036:013 And he made fifty taches of gold, and coupled the curtains one
unto another with the taches: so it became one tabernacle.

02:036:014 And he made curtains of goats' hair for the tent over the
tabernacle: eleven curtains he made them.

02:036:015 The length of one curtain was thirty cubits, and four cubits

was the breadth of one curtain: the eleven curtains were of
one size.

02:036:016 And he coupled five curtains by themselves, and six curtains by themselves.

02:036:017 And he made fifty loops upon the uttermost edge of the curtain in the coupling, and fifty loops made he upon the edge of the curtain which coupleth the second.

02:036:018 And he made fifty taches of brass to couple the tent together, that it might be one.

02:036:019 And he made a covering for the tent of rams' skins dyed red, and a covering of badgers' skins above that.

02:036:020 And he made boards for the tabernacle of shittim wood, standing up.

02:036:021 The length of a board was ten cubits, and the breadth of a board one cubit and a half.

02:036:022 One board had two tenons, equally distant one from another: thus did he make for all the boards of the tabernacle.

02:036:023 And he made boards for the tabernacle; twenty boards for the south side southward:

02:036:024 And forty sockets of silver he made under the twenty boards; two sockets under one board for his two tenons, and two sockets under another board for his two tenons.

02:036:025 And for the other side of the tabernacle, which is toward the north corner, he made twenty boards,

02:036:026 And their forty sockets of silver; two sockets under one board, and two sockets under another board.

02:036:027 And for the sides of the tabernacle westward he made six boards.

02:036:028 And two boards made he for the corners of the tabernacle in the two sides.

02:036:029 And they were coupled beneath, and coupled together at the head thereof, to one ring: thus he did to both of them in both the corners.

02:036:030 And there were eight boards; and their sockets were sixteen sockets of silver, under every board two sockets.

02:036:031 And he made bars of shittim wood; five for the boards of the one side of the tabernacle,

02:036:032 And five bars for the boards of the other side of the tabernacle, and five bars for the boards of the tabernacle for the sides westward.

02:036:033 And he made the middle bar to shoot through the boards from the one end to the other.

02:036:034 And he overlaid the boards with gold, and made their rings of gold to be places for the bars, and overlaid the bars with gold.

02:036:035 And he made a vail of blue, and purple, and scarlet, and fine twined linen: with cherubims made he it of cunning work.

02:036:036 And he made thereunto four pillars of shittim wood, and overlaid them with gold: their hooks were of gold; and he cast for them four sockets of silver.

02:036:037 And he made an hanging for the tabernacle door of blue, and purple, and scarlet, and fine twined linen, of needlework;

02:036:038 And the five pillars of it with their hooks: and he overlaid their chapiters and their fillets with gold: but their five sockets were of brass.

02:037:001 And Bezaleel made the ark of shittim wood: two cubits and a half was the length of it, and a cubit and a half the breadth of it, and a cubit and a half the height of it:

02:037:002 And he overlaid it with pure gold within and without, and made a crown of gold to it round about.

02:037:003 And he cast for it four rings of gold, to be set by the four corners of it; even two rings upon the one side of it, and two rings upon the other side of it.

02:037:004 And he made staves of shittim wood, and overlaid them with gold.

02:037:005 And he put the staves into the rings by the sides of the ark, to bear the ark.

02:037:006 And he made the mercy seat of pure gold: two cubits and a half was the length thereof, and one cubit and a half the breadth thereof.

02:037:007 And he made two cherubims of gold, beaten out of one piece made he them, on the two ends of the mercy seat;

02:037:008 One cherub on the end on this side, and another cherub on the other end on that side: out of the mercy seat made he the cherubims on the two ends thereof.

02:037:009 And the cherubims spread out their wings on high, and covered with their wings over the mercy seat, with their faces one to another; even to the mercy seatward were the faces of the cherubims.

02:037:010 And he made the table of shittim wood: two cubits was the length thereof, and a cubit the breadth thereof, and a cubit and a half the height thereof:

02:037:011 And he overlaid it with pure gold, and made thereunto a crown of gold round about.

02:037:012 Also he made thereunto a border of an handbreadth round about; and made a crown of gold for the border thereof round about.

02:037:013 And he cast for it four rings of gold, and put the rings upon the four corners that were in the four feet thereof.

02:037:014 Over against the border were the rings, the places for the staves to bear the table.

02:037:015 And he made the staves of shittim wood, and overlaid them with gold, to bear the table.

02:037:016 And he made the vessels which were upon the table, his dishes, and his spoons, and his bowls, and his covers to cover withal, of pure gold.

02:037:017 And he made the candlestick of pure gold: of beaten work made he the candlestick; his shaft, and his branch, his bowls, his knops, and his flowers, were of the same:

02:037:018 And six branches going out of the sides thereof; three branches of the candlestick out of the one side thereof, and three branches of the candlestick out of the other side thereof:

02:037:019 Three bowls made after the fashion of almonds in one branch, a knop and a flower; and three bowls made like almonds in another branch, a knop and a flower: so throughout the six branches going out of the candlestick.

02:037:020 And in the candlestick were four bowls made like almonds, his knops, and his flowers:

02:037:021 And a knop under two branches of the same, and a knop under two branches of the same, and a knop under two branches of the same, according to the six branches going out of it.

02:037:022 Their knops and their branches were of the same: all of it was one beaten work of pure gold.

02:037:023 And he made his seven lamps, and his snuffers, and his snuffdishes, of pure gold.

02:037:024 Of a talent of pure gold made he it, and all the vessels thereof.

02:037:025 And he made the incense altar of shittim wood: the length of it was a cubit, and the breadth of it a cubit; it was foursquare; and two cubits was the height of it; the horns thereof were of the same.

02:037:026 And he overlaid it with pure gold, both the top of it, and the sides thereof round about, and the horns of it: also he made unto it a crown of gold round about.

02:037:027 And he made two rings of gold for it under the crown thereof, by the two corners of it, upon the two sides thereof, to be places for the staves to bear it withal.

02:037:028 And he made the staves of shittim wood, and overlaid them with gold.

02:037:029 And he made the holy anointing oil, and the pure incense of sweet spices, according to the work of the apothecary.

02:038:001 And he made the altar of burnt offering of shittim wood: five cubits was the length thereof, and five cubits the breadth thereof; it was foursquare; and three cubits the height thereof.

02:038:002 And he made the horns thereof on the four corners of it; the horns thereof were of the same: and he overlaid it with brass.

02:038:003 And he made all the vessels of the altar, the pots, and the shovels, and the basons, and the fleshhooks, and the firepans: all the vessels thereof made he of brass.

02:038:004 And he made for the altar a brasen grate of network under the compass thereof beneath unto the midst of it.

02:038:005 And he cast four rings for the four ends of the grate of
brass, to be places for the staves.

02:038:006 And he made the staves of shittim wood, and overlaid them with
brass.

02:038:007 And he put the staves into the rings on the sides of the
altar, to bear it withal; he made the altar hollow with
boards.

02:038:008 And he made the laver of brass, and the foot of it of brass,
of the lookingglasses of the women assembling, which assembled
at the door of the tabernacle of the congregation.

02:038:009 And he made the court: on the south side southward the
hangings of the court were of fine twined linen, an hundred
cubits:

02:038:010 Their pillars were twenty, and their brasen sockets twenty;
the hooks of the pillars and their fillets were of silver.

02:038:011 And for the north side the hangings were an hundred cubits,
their pillars were twenty, and their sockets of brass twenty;
the hooks of the pillars and their fillets of silver.

02:038:012 And for the west side were hangings of fifty cubits, their
pillars ten, and their sockets ten; the hooks of the pillars
and their fillets of silver.

02:038:013 And for the east side eastward fifty cubits.

02:038:014 The hangings of the one side of the gate were fifteen cubits;
their pillars three, and their sockets three.

02:038:015 And for the other side of the court gate, on this hand and
that hand, were hangings of fifteen cubits; their pillars
three, and their sockets three.

02:038:016 All the hangings of the court round about were of fine twined linen.

02:038:017 And the sockets for the pillars were of brass; the hooks of
the pillars and their fillets of silver; and the overlaying of
their chapiters of silver; and all the pillars of the court
were filleted with silver.

02:038:018 And the hanging for the gate of the court was needlework, of
blue, and purple, and scarlet, and fine twined linen: and
twenty cubits was the length, and the height in the breadth
was five cubits, answerable to the hangings of the court.

02:038:019 And their pillars were four, and their sockets of brass four;
their hooks of silver, and the overlaying of their chapiters
and their fillets of silver.

02:038:020 And all the pins of the tabernacle, and of the court round
about, were of brass.

02:038:021 This is the sum of the tabernacle, even of the tabernacle of
testimony, as it was counted, according to the commandment of
Moses, for the service of the Levites, by the hand of Ithamar,
son to Aaron the priest.

02:038:022 And Bezaleel the son Uri, the son of Hur, of the tribe of
Judah, made all that the LORD commanded Moses.

02:038:023 And with him was Aholiab, son of Ahisamach, of the tribe of
Dan, an engraver, and a cunning workman, and an embroiderer in
blue, and in purple, and in scarlet, and fine linen.

02:038:024 All the gold that was occupied for the work in all the work of
the holy place, even the gold of the offering, was twenty and
nine talents, and seven hundred and thirty shekels, after the
shekel of the sanctuary.

02:038:025 And the silver of them that were numbered of the congregation
was an hundred talents, and a thousand seven hundred and
threescore and fifteen shekels, after the shekel of the

sanctuary:

02:038:026 A bekah for every man, that is, half a shekel, after the
shekel of the sanctuary, for every one that went to be
numbered, from twenty years old and upward, for six hundred
thousand and three thousand and five hundred and fifty men.

02:038:027 And of the hundred talents of silver were cast the sockets of
the sanctuary, and the sockets of the vail; an hundred sockets
of the hundred talents, a talent for a socket.

02:038:028 And of the thousand seven hundred seventy and five shekels he
made hooks for the pillars, and overlaid their chapiters, and
filleted them.

02:038:029 And the brass of the offering was seventy talents, and two
thousand and four hundred shekels.

02:038:030 And therewith he made the sockets to the door of the
tabernacle of the congregation, and the brasen altar, and the
brasen grate for it, and all the vessels of the altar,

02:038:031 And the sockets of the court round about, and the sockets of
the court gate, and all the pins of the tabernacle, and all
the pins of the court round about.

02:039:001 And of the blue, and purple, and scarlet, they made cloths of
service, to do service in the holy place, and made the holy
garments for Aaron; as the LORD commanded Moses.

02:039:002 And he made the ephod of gold, blue, and purple, and scarlet,
and fine twined linen.

02:039:003 And they did beat the gold into thin plates, and cut it into
wires, to work it in the blue, and in the purple, and in the
scarlet, and in the fine linen, with cunning work.

02:039:004 They made shoulderpieces for it, to couple it together: by the
two edges was it coupled together.

02:039:005 And the curious girdle of his ephod, that was upon it, was of
the same, according to the work thereof; of gold, blue, and
purple, and scarlet, and fine twined linen; as the LORD
commanded Moses.

02:039:006 And they wrought onyx stones inclosed in ouches of gold,
graven, as signets are graven, with the names of the children
of Israel.

02:039:007 And he put them on the shoulders of the ephod, that they
should be stones for a memorial to the children of Israel; as
the LORD commanded Moses.

02:039:008 And he made the breastplate of cunning work, like the work of
the ephod; of gold, blue, and purple, and scarlet, and fine
twined linen.

02:039:009 It was foursquare; they made the breastplate double: a span
was the length thereof, and a span the breadth thereof, being
doubled.

02:039:010 And they set in it four rows of stones: the first row was a
sardius, a topaz, and a carbuncle: this was the first row.

02:039:011 And the second row, an emerald, a sapphire, and a diamond.

02:039:012 And the third row, a ligure, an agate, and an amethyst.

02:039:013 And the fourth row, a beryl, an onyx, and a jasper: they were
inclosed in ouches of gold in their inclosings.

02:039:014 And the stones were according to the names of the children of
Israel, twelve, according to their names, like the engravings
of a signet, every one with his name, according to the twelve
tribes.

02:039:015 And they made upon the breastplate chains at the ends, of
wreathen work of pure gold.

02:039:016 And they made two ouches of gold, and two gold rings; and put the two rings in the two ends of the breastplate.

02:039:017 And they put the two wreathen chains of gold in the two rings on the ends of the breastplate.

02:039:018 And the two ends of the two wreathen chains they fastened in the two ouches, and put them on the shoulderpieces of the ephod, before it.

02:039:019 And they made two rings of gold, and put them on the two ends of the breastplate, upon the border of it, which was on the side of the ephod inward.

02:039:020 And they made two other golden rings, and put them on the two sides of the ephod underneath, toward the forepart of it, over against the other coupling thereof, above the curious girdle of the ephod.

02:039:021 And they did bind the breastplate by his rings unto the rings of the ephod with a lace of blue, that it might be above the curious girdle of the ephod, and that the breastplate might not be loosed from the ephod; as the LORD commanded Moses.

02:039:022 And he made the robe of the ephod of woven work, all of blue.

02:039:023 And there was an hole in the midst of the robe, as the hole of an habergeon, with a band round about the hole, that it should not rend.

02:039:024 And they made upon the hems of the robe pomegranates of blue, and purple, and scarlet, and twined linen.

02:039:025 And they made bells of pure gold, and put the bells between the pomegranates upon the hem of the robe, round about between the pomegranates;

02:039:026 A bell and a pomegranate, a bell and a pomegranate, round about the hem of the robe to minister in; as the LORD commanded Moses.

02:039:027 And they made coats of fine linen of woven work for Aaron, and for his sons,

02:039:028 And a mitre of fine linen, and goodly bonnets of fine linen, and linen breeches of fine twined linen,

02:039:029 And a girdle of fine twined linen, and blue, and purple, and scarlet, of needlework; as the LORD commanded Moses.

02:039:030 And they made the plate of the holy crown of pure gold, and wrote upon it a writing, like to the engravings of a signet,
HOLINESS TO THE LORD.

02:039:031 And they tied unto it a lace of blue, to fasten it on high upon the mitre; as the LORD commanded Moses.

02:039:032 Thus was all the work of the tabernacle of the tent of the congregation finished: and the children of Israel did
according to all that the LORD commanded Moses, so did they.

02:039:033 And they brought the tabernacle unto Moses, the tent, and all his furniture, his taches, his boards, his bars, and his
pillars, and his sockets,

02:039:034 And the covering of rams' skins dyed red, and the covering of badgers' skins, and the vail of the covering,

02:039:035 The ark of the testimony, and the staves thereof, and the mercy seat,

02:039:036 The table, and all the vessels thereof, and the shewbread,

02:039:037 The pure candlestick, with the lamps thereof, even with the lamps to be set in order, and all the vessels thereof, and the
oil for light,

02:039:038 And the golden altar, and the anointing oil, and the sweet incense, and the hanging for the tabernacle door,

02:039:039 The brasen altar, and his grate of brass, his staves, and all his vessels, the laver and his foot,

02:039:040 The hangings of the court, his pillars, and his sockets, and the hanging for the court gate, his cords, and his pins, and all the vessels of the service of the tabernacle, for the tent of the congregation,

02:039:041 The cloths of service to do service in the holy place, and the holy garments for Aaron the priest, and his sons' garments, to minister in the priest's office.

02:039:042 According to all that the LORD commanded Moses, so the children of Israel made all the work.

02:039:043 And Moses did look upon all the work, and, behold, they had done it as the LORD had commanded, even so had they done it: and Moses blessed them.

02:040:001 And the LORD spake unto Moses, saying,

02:040:002 On the first day of the first month shalt thou set up the tabernacle of the tent of the congregation.

02:040:003 And thou shalt put therein the ark of the testimony, and cover the ark with the vail.

02:040:004 And thou shalt bring in the table, and set in order the things that are to be set in order upon it; and thou shalt bring in the candlestick, and light the lamps thereof.

02:040:005 And thou shalt set the altar of gold for the incense before the ark of the testimony, and put the hanging of the door to the tabernacle.

02:040:006 And thou shalt set the altar of the burnt offering before the door of the tabernacle of the tent of the congregation.

02:040:007 And thou shalt set the laver between the tent of the congregation and the altar, and shalt put water therein.

02:040:008 And thou shalt set up the court round about, and hang up the hanging at the court gate.

02:040:009 And thou shalt take the anointing oil, and anoint the tabernacle, and all that is therein, and shalt hallow it, and all the vessels thereof: and it shall be holy.

02:040:010 And thou shalt anoint the altar of the burnt offering, and all his vessels, and sanctify the altar: and it shall be an altar most holy.

02:040:011 And thou shalt anoint the laver and his foot, and sanctify it.

02:040:012 And thou shalt bring Aaron and his sons unto the door of the tabernacle of the congregation, and wash them with water.

02:040:013 And thou shalt put upon Aaron the holy garments, and anoint him, and sanctify him; that he may minister unto me in the priest's office.

02:040:014 And thou shalt bring his sons, and clothe them with coats:

02:040:015 And thou shalt anoint them, as thou didst anoint their father, that they may minister unto me in the priest's office: for their anointing shall surely be an everlasting priesthood throughout their generations.

02:040:016 Thus did Moses: according to all that the LORD commanded him, so did he.

02:040:017 And it came to pass in the first month in the second year, on the first day of the month, that the tabernacle was reared up.

02:040:018 And Moses reared up the tabernacle, and fastened his sockets, and set up the boards thereof, and put in the bars thereof, and reared up his pillars.

02:040:019 And he spread abroad the tent over the tabernacle, and put the covering of the tent above upon it; as the LORD commanded Moses.

02:040:020 And he took and put the testimony into the ark, and set the staves on the ark, and put the mercy seat above upon the ark:

02:040:021 And he brought the ark into the tabernacle, and set up the vail of the covering, and covered the ark of the testimony; as the LORD commanded Moses.

02:040:022 And he put the table in the tent of the congregation, upon the side of the tabernacle northward, without the vail.

02:040:023 And he set the bread in order upon it before the LORD; as the LORD had commanded Moses.

02:040:024 And he put the candlestick in the tent of the congregation, over against the table, on the side of the tabernacle southward.

02:040:025 And he lighted the lamps before the LORD; as the LORD commanded Moses.

02:040:026 And he put the golden altar in the tent of the congregation before the vail:

02:040:027 And he burnt sweet incense thereon; as the LORD commanded Moses.

02:040:028 And he set up the hanging at the door of the tabernacle.

02:040:029 And he put the altar of burnt offering by the door of the tabernacle of the tent of the congregation, and offered upon it the burnt offering and the meat offering; as the LORD commanded Moses.

02:040:030 And he set the laver between the tent of the congregation and the altar, and put water there, to wash withal.

02:040:031 And Moses and Aaron and his sons washed their hands and their feet thereat:

02:040:032 When they went into the tent of the congregation, and when they came near unto the altar, they washed; as the LORD commanded Moses.

02:040:033 And he reared up the court round about the tabernacle and the altar, and set up the hanging of the court gate. So Moses finished the work.

02:040:034 Then a cloud covered the tent of the congregation, and the glory of the LORD filled the tabernacle.

02:040:035 And Moses was not able to enter into the tent of the congregation, because the cloud abode thereon, and the glory of the LORD filled the tabernacle.

02:040:036 And when the cloud was taken up from over the tabernacle, the children of Israel went onward in all their journeys:

02:040:037 But if the cloud were not taken up, then they journeyed not till the day that it was taken up.

02:040:038 For the cloud of the LORD was upon the tabernacle by day, and fire was on it by night, in the sight of all the house of Israel, throughout all their journeys.

CPSIA information can be obtained at www.ICGtesting.com
233249LV00002B/59/P

9 781407 647180